George Tremlett has been a rock writer almost since the music began in the mid-Fifties. He left King Edward VI School, Stratford-upon-Avon, in 1957 and then spent four years on *The Coventry Evening Telegraph* writing their daily TV column and reviewing all the visiting pop package shows.

In 1961 he moved to London and became a freelance writer, working part-time for *The New Musical Express*. He has since been London correspondent for TV and pop music magazines in Japan, Holland, Belgium, Germany, Australia, New Zealand, Finland, Sweden, and the United States. In this he is partnered by his wife, Jane. They also contribute to most major British teenage magazines.

Outside pop music journalism, George Tremlett pursues a political career as a member of the Greater London Council. For the past eleven years he has also been a councillor in Richmond-upon-Thames.

Also by George Tremlett

THE DAVID BOWIE STORY

George Tremlett

The Osmond Story

Futura Publications Limited

A Futura Book

First published in Great Britain in 1974
by Futura Publications Limited

ISBN 0 8600 7027 1
Printed in Great Britain by
C. Nicholls & Company Ltd.
The Philips Park Press
Manchester.

Futura Publications Limited,
49 Poland Street,
LONDON W1A 2LG

ACKNOWLEDGEMENTS

In writing this book, I am especially grateful to Mr. and Mrs. George Osmond who spent several hours discussing their family with me, and the remarkable way their children had been brought up. Originally my intention was to use this material for a series of articles, but as our last conversation ended, Mr. Osmond said, "You've got enough there for a book." He proved to be right, though I have also drawn on my own conversations with Alan, Wayne, Merrill, Jay, Donny and Jimmy, and upon my wife Jane's two interviews with their sister Marie. I am also particularly grateful to Mrs. Maureen Street, secretary of the Osmonds' British fan club.

CHAPTER ONE

In just two years, the Osmonds have become the First Family of Pop. Never before has one family been so successful and so predominant in so many areas of the music business, appealing to such different age groups. Between them, George and Olive Osmond and their nine children include four major world recording acts, each selling records by the million and on every Continent – and yet even this is only one aspect of their phenomenal story.

Within the Osmond family, there is also a team of songwriters, a record producer, an engineer, three solo singers – plus a host of affiliated businesses and investments that include holdings in real estate and such strange by-products as Marie Osmond Cosmetics, "Mrs. Osmond's Family Cookbook", a monthly magazine in Britain "Osmond's World" and a 2,300-acre ranch at Wartske, Utah, where by careful breeding they have now reached the second generation in establishing their own herd of pedigree Simmental cattle, an all-white breed that originated in Switzerland.

Musically, the Osmonds in their various permutations have an extraordinary track record. There is the group The Osmonds – comprising the five brothers Jay, Merrill, Alan, Wayne and Donny – which appeared regularly on the Andy Williams TV series in the United States (and syndicated around the world), and has since developed into a choreographed stage act with its own backing band, appearing annually at Caesar's Palace in Las Vegas. They have toured Europe, Australasia and

Japan, and have had a run of multi-million selling singles like "Hold Her Tight", "Crazy Horses", "Goin' Home" and "Let Me In" plus best-selling albums such as "Phase III", "The Osmonds Live", "Crazy Horses" and "The Plan".

Then Donny, the youngest of the group, he of the dark brown hair and teeth so perfect, has become Britain's No. 1 teenage heart-throb, has made young hearts flutter from Wigan to Alice Springs, teaching teenage magazine editors that they only have to print a colour portrait of him on their covers (or, better still, offer a large-as-life pull-out poster), and they may increase their weekly print order by as much as 100,000. His is the face that has papered so many bedroom walls – a quality, combined with his work as a singer, that has enabled Donny to sell more than a million copies of every one of his singles – "Sweet and Innocent", "Go Away Little Girl", "Hey Girl", "Puppy Love", "Too Young", "Why", "The Twelfth of Never", "Young Love" and "When I Fall in Love". In some cases, he has sold many times that – meaning that by the time Donny was sixteen years old his income from royalties was probably twenty times the annual salary of the U.S. President.

And then there are the younger children who only make occasional stage and TV appearances with their elder brothers – Jimmy and Marie. Since he was five years old, Jimmy has been a major recording artist in Japan. Before the age of ten, he had a No. 1 hit single in Britain, "Long Haired Lover From Liverpool" – and before his eleventh birthday he had been included in a list of the top 140 income-earners in the United States.

Even sister Marie, the only girl in the Osmond family, graduated to the Charts in 1973, giving up her earlier and more worldly ambitions to be a shorthand typist –

and went straight to No. 1 in the United States with her first single, a country and western-style song "Paper Roses", which has since been a hit in Britain.

All that, impressive though it may seem, is only the beginning of the story. The Osmonds also have all those associated business enterprises, which underline their wealth and total control of every aspect of their professional careers. Even before they started making hit records, their father George Osmond had invested the income from their TV series in the 2,300-acre ranch at Wartske, where their farm staff keep the Osmonds' own private stable of twenty five horses – plus that herd of cattle.

Now, with their vastly increased income over the past two years, the family have invested in office blocks and apartment buildings. They have erected their own private recording studios – not one, but two. These are administered by their own recording company, Kolob, with one studio in Los Angeles and the other at Provo, Utah, where the Osmonds now have their main home actually on the campus of the Brigham Young University (they also have other homes at Ogden, Utah (where-most of them were born), at Los Angeles, and at Wartske).

"They are the finest studios I have ever seen – with superb equipment, as well fitted as any of the major American recording companies," says Mick Flinn of Springfield Revival, one of the few groups to have recorded there other than the Osmonds themselves.

And then there are the enterprises that have developed under the Osmonds' wing – the range of organic cosmetics marketed under Marie's name in the States, and shortly to be distributed in Europe as well; the cookery book compiled by Mrs. Osmond and enabling her sons' fans to not only buy their records but even share the same diet; the magazine "Osmonds World", which details every facet of their progress, covering their tours and TV shows, their recording sessions, their journeys abroad, their religion and family history, and then there is the fan club, which is no ordinary fan club.

Most fan clubs exist for two purposes – firstly to give the fans an opportunity to have direct contact with their idols, often meeting them, getting autographs, and personal information about their lives and their careers which might not be printed in the music papers or teenage magazines. But from the artists' point of view, and particularly that of their managers, the fan clubs serve another purpose – they provide a major vehicle for promotion, a means of guaranteeing that thousands of requests will flood into the radio station offices asking for singles and tracks from albums to be played. The fans are always told when new records are being released so that they can sit down, write out their postcard requests – and thereby boost the popularity (and, of course), the income of their favourite star. Some fan clubs even notify their members of impending popularity polls in the music press so that the fans can rush out to buy extra copies of that week's issue to plug their idol – which can again be an important financial boost to the artist because success in such polls will impress pop music's entrepreneurs.

But the Osmonds' Fan Club is much different to this, organised on a vast scale in Europe and in the United States – with the American side of it being personally supervised by the Osmonds' two elder brothers, Virl and Tommy, who were both born with impaired hearing and thus cannot be in music themselves (which explains why every member of the Osmond family right down to little Jimmy can communicate across a crowded room in deaf and dumb language, and why they have also invested a large part of their income in a charity, the Osmonds Foundation For The Deaf, which finances research into the causes of deafness, and helps young children so afflicted).

The American fan club has approx 60,000 members, who all pay a subscription of three dollars a year. Then the European Fan Club, which is run by a North London housewife Mrs. Maureen Street, whose husband is a music publisher, has nearly 70,000 members, who pay an annual subscription of 75 pence a year. For this they receive four quarterly newsletters with up to date information on every member of the Osmonds' family (including details of their choice in clothes, toothpaste, food; their beliefs as members of the Mormon Church; their pets; their medical history, their neck and waist measurements, the size of their shoes, the condition of their teeth and even their weight at birth), a short biography of the group, a colour photo, a metal pin-on badge, an 8 in. x 5 in. signed photo and a membership card. Occasionally, there will be a special gift for all members – at Christmas 1973 they all received a "personal Christmas message", recorded specially by the Osmonds in Utah, and then recorded as a "flimsy". With the newsletters, fans also receive details of the different products available to them as they are to members of the American fan club – and this is where the Osmonds merchandising operation comes into play.

The devoted fan can receive a ten per cent discount on all her long playing records, special imports of American records, and a vast range of Osmond "goodies" – which include T-shirts, scarves, velvet caps, pillow cases, writing pads, key rings, tote bags, song books, bracelets, medallions.

To be fair, the prices compare favourably with those elsewhere – and items like song books are sold at lower prices than fans would have to pay in the shops. The Osmonds make no money out of their fan club because they do give better value and more detailed newsletters (sometimes running to six or eight closely printed foolscap pages) than other fan clubs. They do offer more to members than is usual – and they are much better organised than any fan club has been since the halcyon days of The Beatles. The Osmonds Fan Club members are made to feel that they really do belong, that the Osmonds care about them – which they undoubtedly do because every single gift, every birthday card, every Christmas card that Maureen Street receives is air-freighted to Utah.

"We make no profit out of the fan club – but it does pay for itself," says Mrs. Street. That in itself is unusual – some fan clubs run at a loss because artists and their managers appreciate the benefits that come from subsidising 2-3,000 devoted fans who will dutifully sit down and compile their postcard requests as soon as the latest newsletter drops on the mat. (The royalties that come from the Performing Rights Society for radio plays comprise a major part of most artists' incomes.)

But what is even more extraordinary is the close intimacy that a member of the fan club is genuinely able to achieve with the Osmonds – often learning more about them and their daily lives, the way they organise themselves, relax, furnish their homes and go about their work, than they ever would about neighbours living in the same street.

This is all part of the image that the Osmonds have projected in their travels across the States, across Australasia and the Far East, through the capitals of Europe and throughout Britain – the image summed up in George Osmond's phrase that "the family that plays together stays together". Wherever work takes them, they go together, forming one great big happy family – with fans genuinely believing that if they join the Fan Club they, too, become part of something larger than themselves. If this was insincere, it would be a most callous exercise. But it is not. The Osmonds believe in the roles they play; they are themselves in all they do – which makes every tiny detail of their lives public.

CHAPTER TWO

The first time the Osmond family visited London in May, 1972, Mrs. Olive Osmond came here with a special purpose. She wanted to have her ancestors recognised as Saints. This may sound strange to anyone not a member of the Osmond family faith, the Church of Jesus Christ of Latter Day Saints, more commonly known as "the Mormons", a strict sect based in Salt Lake City, Utah. For many years, the Mormons practised polygamy and were almost a separate society within the United States, basing their religion on the teachings of Brigham Young and the messages contained in the Book of Mormon.

In recent years, polygamy has ceased to be practised there. But the religion is still strict – with its members barred from drinking tea and coffee as well as alcohol and Coca Cola on the grounds that they contain artificial stimulants. At the Brigham Young University in Provo, Utah, where the Osmonds have their home actually on the university campus, long hair is frowned upon. Rules are strict. Pre-marital sex is not tolerated. Marriage itself is regarded as everlasting.

It is an important part of the Mormon faith that all the ancestors of any living Mormon can – if their ancestry is established – become "Latter Day Saints", i.e. the living can elect the dead members of the Church. To Mrs. Osmond this was very important because the whole family had been brought up within the Mormon faith. Her husband, George Osmond, had been a Bishop of the Church in the town of Ogden, Utah, before the Osmonds started their careers in the entertainment business, a man respected as a leading citizen, a pillar of local society, bringing his children up with the same basic beliefs and attitudes.

Indeed, his children started their careers in show business by performing at Mormon church functions – and it was on a tour of Mormon churches in California, when they took a day off to visit Disneyland, that they were first discovered by a Disney executive, who offered them a spot on a TV show, which was in turn seen by Andy Williams' father, who knew that his son was looking for a young singing act to appear on the weekly TV series that he was shortly scheduled to begin. And it was from that that the Osmond TV and singing career began.

So in a very real way, it could be said that the Osmonds owed everything they had to the Mormons, and they have continued to be devout practising members of that religion, living to high moral precepts – and never allowing any drop of any artificial stimulant to enter their bodies (though Donny did once, by mistake, sip a can of shandy with two per cent alcohol!) Likewise, they eat only organically produced vegetables. They never use bad language – and every Sunday they always visit the nearest Mormon church and participate in the services. (When staying in London, they have visited Mormon churches in Bayswater and in Sussex).

With such a background, only one thing was missing – they had not established their family tree. All the family records taken over to America by the first George Osmond to emigrate from London in the early 19th century had been destroyed in a fire. Since then, they had tried to re-trace the records, but all avenues of research had been exhausted. Vital pieces of information were missing from the late 18th and early 19th century records of births, marriages and deaths – and so, as a family, they had hardly any Saints.

This is very important to a Mormon – so much so that nearly all the parish registers in Britain have been microfilmed, and then the films taken to Salt Lake City, where there is a massive master index to which any Mormon anxious to trace his ancestry may refer – which they do, in their thousands.

Now, I happened to know all this because the previous year I had been undertaking some genealogical research work myself, and had learnt how to unravel family trees, how to search through the registers of births, marriages and deaths at Somerset House, how to trace records back beyond 1837 (when the first registers were assembled at Somerset House) through the archives of the Genealogical Society in Harrington Gardens, Kensington, with the aid of Boyd's Marriage Index (which contains tens of thousands of marriage details from the mid-16th century onwards), and how to track down through local parish registers details that might be missing elsewhere. All this was new to Mrs. Osmond who was not aware how genealogical research could be done in this country, and who was (and still is) desperately anxious to trace back the family ancestry so that all the Osmond forefathers could be recognised as Saints. "You probably don't realise how important all this is to us," she told me, when we had our first long conversation at the Churchill Hotel in London.

"As Mormons, we believe it is essential to trace your ancestry .... I've had researchers working on this in Salt Lake City for years, but there are all sorts of gaps ... many of our own family records are missing. There was a fire at one of the family houses many years ago, and all the certificates that had been brought over to America by the first Osmonds to emigrate from London were destroyed. . . . so we have nothing to start with . . . we no longer have the leads that would tell us which part of England they lived in before moving to London."

I gave Mrs. Osmond the address of the Genealogical Society, and suggested she approach them – if not to do the work herself, then to ask if they could recommend someone who would trace the family tree for her for a fee, and I also gave her the addresses of several people and organisations in this country who make their profession tracing family histories.

The name "Osmond" itself has the most interesting derivation, with direct religious meanings. It is one of the oldest names in Britain with a history going back far beyond the Norman invasion.

In "The Origin of English Surnames" (published by Routledge and Kegan Paul in 1967), P. H. Reaney reveals that Osmond was originally an Old English personal name – one by which someone was known before the adoption of surnames. Indeed, he records that in the 8th century there was a King of Sussex with the name Osmund – a spelling used frequently in the Domesday Book.

Another researcher Henry Harrington said in his book "Surnames of the United Kingdom" (published in 1912 by the Eaton Press) that Osmond was basically Anglo Saxon. It was a name partly English and partly Scandinavian in origin. The first part of the name "Os" was the word for a God, and the second "mund" meant hand or protector. Thus the meaning of the word Osmond was "divine protector". He recorded that one Osmund was consecrated Bishop of Salisbury in 1078 and died in 1099, and that he was believed to have been created Earl of Dorset around 1070 – though the documentary evidence of this has not been found. According to one source published by the Wiltshire Record Society in 1901, this Osmund was a nephew of William the Conqueror, being son of Henry, Count of Seez by Isabella, daughter of Robert, Duke of Normandy. In those days, the population of Sussex could only have been a thousand or two so there is a possibility that the Osmonds could, if they were able to trace their ancestry, go back a very long way indeed since it was customary for surnames to be taken from personal names that had been used in families for generations. Certainly, whatever their origins, they would seem to have one of the oldest names in the English language.

Until the summer of 1972, the Osmond family of Ogden, Utah, had never been to Britain – though they knew that their great grandfather had been a London-born lawyer who had emigrated to the States, and that prior to that the family had been English for as far back as family legend travels. Once, Mrs. Osmond told me, she had looked up a London telephone directory while she was back home in Utah, had seen an Osmond in the book. "So I wrote to them out of the blue," she said. "That was Terence Osmond and his wife Hilda, and we started writing to each other, almost like pen pals.... and I kept this up for about twelve years, exchanging letters two or three times a year, and then Hilda told me just before we arrived here that Terence had died. We'd never met, but we'd dearly loved to have met him because we'd like to find our relatives.... I'd like to be able to publish our family pedigree."

She told me that they knew that her husband's father Rulon Osmond had been born in Afton, Wyoming, on August 17, 1893, and that his father George Osmond – the great grandfather of Donny and his brothers – had been a Londoner, born in London on May 23, 1836, and that his father had also been a Londoner, with the same name, George Osmond, born somewhere around 1800. "But we can't find where he was born," she said.

"It all gets very hard to disentangle. So far as we can tell, that first George Osmond had a twin brother called John, and he married a Nancy Ann Canham, who herself later married George Osmond ... but something must have gone wrong with that marriage. We know they married, but something happened to it – they must have been divorced or something.... we've managed to trace his will, and he left all his money to someone called Martha Scarsbruck, who was his housekeeper.... and apparently Nancy then married someone called Hanson Flight, and she had some children because George knows that his grandfather had a half-sister called Rosabella Crocker in this country while he was living out in the States.... I can't tell you how much money we have spent trying to sort all this out. It runs into hundreds of dollars. We've looked through the microfilms at Salt Lake City, and written countless letters, but we haven't been able to sort it out.... I've employed a geneaologist, and I've written to Somerset House, but it is all just as big a mystery to us now as it was when we first started trying to work it all out."

Her own side of the family tree is much less complicated, and has proved relatively easy to establish. Mrs Osmond knows that all eight of her great grandparents were born in Britain, and that on her father's side they were all Welsh, from the mining valleys of Camarthen and Glamorgan. They were all evidently of hardy stock because all eight emigrated to the United States somewhere around the 1860's, and it was there that all four of her grandparents were born – three of them in Utah and the fourth in Pennsylvania.

Her own father Thomas Martin Davis was a farmer in Samaria, Idaho, coupling this with another job as County Superintendent for the local education authority. There, she grew up with her brother Tom. Later, their parents sold the farm and the family moved to Ogden, Utah, where she worked during the war as a secretary at a U.S. military base. It was while working there that she first met George Osmond, who had returned home to Ogden after three years' Army service during which he had been stationed at Brentwood, Essex, and also at Exeter in Devon.

He was then an almost confirmed bachelor, with no thoughts of marriage – even though he was already twenty six years old.

"I had enjoyed myself in England, and had no immediate intentions of getting married when I returned home to Ogden," Mr. Osmond told me. "I was very happy with my life as it was."

But then he and Olive met, and found they had so much to share – even to the extent that he was born in Star Valley, Wyoming, where Olive's mother had been a school teacher before her own marriage, boarding with the Osmond family after George's father Rulon had been killed by a horse while struggling to pull logs out of a canyon. Even before Olive Davis was born, her own mother had cradled Olive's future husband in her arms, had taught him the names of animals as they walked in the woods around the Osmond home.

With so much to remember and so much to talk about, love flourished – and on December 1st, 1944, George Osmond and Olive Davis were married at the Mormon Temple in Salt Lake City, having postponed the wedding date once because of family illness. Afterwards, they held a small reception at her parents' home, and then established their own home in a block of flats in Ogden that had been specially built by the U.S. Government as a wartime housing project.

For the first few months of their marriage, Olive continued working at the Army base – but then she found she was expecting their first baby, and gave up work. Meanwhile, George Osmond was planning to buy his first piece of land and build a home for his family.

Their first son, Tommy, was born on October 25th, 1945; their second, Virl, on October 19th, 1947; their third, Alan Ralph, on June 22nd, 1949; their fourth Wayne on August 28th., 1951; their fifth, Merrill Davis, on April 30th, 1953; their sixth, Jay Wesley, on March 2nd, 1955, and their seventh, Donald Clark, on December 9th, 1957.

By any standards, Mrs. Osmond was to prove a remarkable mother. When she found that her first two sons, Tommy and Virl, had been born with impaired hearing she taught herself deaf and dumb language, then she taught them how to communicate – and she was to later tell Mrs. Maureen Street, secretary of the European Fan Club, that she used a vacuum cleaner to demonstrate to them both the close relationship between vibration and speech. Coming from a family of teachers, she taught Virl and Tommy to speak – and they both later went on to complete degree courses at the Brigham Young University.

Meanwhile, as she concentrated on the home and bringing up her children, George Osmond had become a respected citizen in Ogden. He had moved from one house to another, and always to a better one. Within the Church, he had become a Bishop (which is not the same as being a Bishop in the Church of England – its nearest parallel appears to be membership of a parish council). He had laid down the foundations for a successful business, having built up an insurance agency, also running a post office and dealing in real estate. His had been a very hard-working life with much of the responsibility for bringing up the family being left to Olive, while he made sure the bank account was always kept in a healthy state.

But though he may have been somewhat remote at times with the pressures of his various business activities, George Osmond fully supported his wife in the very firm ideas she had on family life, and on bringing up children – ideas that were to play such an important part in the development of their sons.

All their different homes had large gardens, sometimes fields and orchards – and the houses themselves were carefully chosen so that Mrs. Osmond, with her educational background, could have a private schoolroom for her children.

There, Virl, Tommy, Alan, Wayne, Merrill, Jay and later Donny all had their own desks where they could work on their homework or special family projects, with their own private library of books, electric gadgets to play with, equipment for experiments in physics or chemistry – and a complete range of musical instruments, all kept in a good state of repair. If one of them wanted to learn saxophone, he only had to open the case – and likewise there were trumpets and clarinets, guitars and banjoes, flutes and bass, and even a grand piano.

"I have always thought it very important that children should have the opportunity to create music when they want to," Mrs. Osmond was to tell me years later, explaining that she herself had learned how to play saxophone when she was a girl.

"Likewise, I liked them to have an encyclopaedia so that they could answer any question that came up in their work, dictionaries so that they could check spelling as they went along, paints and brushes so that they could paint and draw when they felt like it. . . . I wanted to encourage them to use their hands, to be creative, and to think for themselves . . . it was something I set out to do, something that started when the boys were all very small.

"At the main house that we had during their childhood, there was a large orchard with apple trees, pears, peaches, plums and greengages so that the boys could grow used to picking fruit when they wanted something to eat – rather than sweets . . . and then we had a vegetable garden where we grew all our own vegetables for the house, and the boys would get used to helping their father turn the soil, sow the seeds, and then reap the crops.

"We had just one cow, Daisy, who was the special responsibility of Virl and Tommy. She was very tame – and she was 'their' cow. They fed her, cleaned out her shed – and then every morning before going to school, they would milk her to provide milk for the family.

"One of the earliest memories I have of Donny is of him when he was still a toddler, sitting on the ground, cross-legged, playing while Virl and Tommy milked Daisy . . . it's just a little picture I have of him in my mind, sitting there.

"Every Fall (an American word for 'autumn'), we would kill a steer and put it in the locker ('deep freeze') to provide us with meat through the winter months . . . in the kitchen I had my own pasteurising equipment so that we could pasteurise the milk that Virl and Tommy brought in, separating off the cream so that we could make our own cheese and butter every week – and special home-made ice cream for the family every Friday evening."

This undisturbed family routine continued throughout the Fifties while Mr. Osmond was hard at his business by day, devoting several evenings a week to church work, administering the church and also helping with pastoral work, charitable work for those who were sick or had fallen on hard times.

"But I'd gradually started to realise that though my wife was doing a marvellous job bringing up the boys, I was really neglecting my family," Mr. Osmond told me. "I was working very, very hard, and there just weren't enough hours in the week for me to do everything that I really needed to do . . . in our Church, we place great emphasis on the need for members of the Church to look after and to be with their families, playing a responsible part in the upbringing of their children, and thinking about my work in the Church made me think about the ways I could reorganise myself. I sat down with Olive and talked about all this, and we came up with our solution."

Mr. Osmond decided to spend part of each weekend with the boys, driving them out into the country in the family car – and to make every Friday evening a special family occasion.

"This became a big thing in our family," said Mr. Osmond. "Every Friday evening, there would be no homework – and instead we would all gather in the dining room for a special dinner by candle light. That evening, Olive and I would devote our whole time to the family. We would begin the evening with prayers, and then we would have dinner – and every week it would be the turn of one of the boys to have as part of the dinner one special dish that he really loved."

Thus one week dinner would include a fruit salad because this was Alan's favourite dish; on another there would be a spaghetti course just to please Wayne; on Merrill's night, his favourite meal of fish and macaroni would be served; Donny would have a special candy which the family called Divinity and which included vanilla ice cream and nuts, and then Jay would have a salad which Mrs. Osmond named "Jay's Einstein Salad" because it contained so many enzymes with its base of vegetables and bean shoots.

"Each of the boys had his special dish, and so each week one of them would have this special treat to look forward to ... Marie was very young at this time, but we'd sit her round the table as well in her high chair and she'd have a special raspberry jelly salad some weeks because that was one of her favourite treats," said Mrs. Osmond.

"They also knew that after we had eaten our dinner, we would push back the table, and then Olive and I would sit down in the easy chairs while the boys entertained us. This became as important a part of Friday evenings as the dinner. During the week, they would be in the school room learning their instruments, writing songs or remembering a song that someone else had written, and then it would be kept a big secret until Friday night when they would play the songs to us.

"Sometimes, they would stage a short play or read some poetry or an extract from a book, sometimes varying it so that they put on a complete show of their own ... and all this was always kept a secret until the Friday. Olive and I never knew what they were planning, and so there was this big build-up of tension during the week, this feeling of excitement in the house as Friday night approached."

The other important feature of the Friday evening timetable was the moment when they sat down to discuss family finances. "I have never believed in pocket money," says Mr. Osmond. I don't believe in the idea of a boy being given a set amount of money each week without any idea how to spend it. . . . I think a boy should learn to plan how he spends his money before he receives it, and that is why none of my children has ever had pocket money.

"Instead on Friday evenings, the boys would all get a special opportunity to make any requests they had for money. Then the rest of us would sit round the table and discuss whether it was a good idea or not . . . thus if Alan wanted to buy a new bike, he would say so. Then the others would talk about it, and the fact that they wanted bikes . . . we would point out that they couldn't all have new bikes at once because of the cost . . . and then we would balance what Alan wanted against what the others might want . . . one of them might point out that Alan was the eldest and therefore he should be the first to have a new bike . . . but if there was something they all wanted to have between them, like a tent to go camping, then that might come first . . . each in turn would have to make his case."

Mrs. Osmond interjected to say that on every occasion where there was a disagreement between the brothers as to who should have the next treat, the matter would be put to a family vote, "with it being accepted that Father had the right to veto anything. He is the Head of the House, the Patriarch – and therefore it's right that he should have the right to veto any project that he thought unwise ... but often there would be no need for this because the boys would come forward with projects they all wanted to share in like buying a boat they could all use, or buying motor cycles for the ranch (we have four of them up at the ranch), or buying snowmobiles to use during the winter when we go up into the mountains to our cabin for Christmas (we had that other home up in the mountains all through their childhood and used to go up there for holidays – and always at Christmas)."

And then Mr. Osmond decided that as well as learning that before spending money they had to justify it, the boys would also benefit by studying more deeply the implications of buying and selling, of capital and income, of using mortgages to buy property.

"We started a family investment project," said Mr. Osmond. "The boys together bought a property on mortgage, and then they let the property off and used the rent income to pay off the mortgage until they had acquired the deeds.

"Every Friday night, we had a progress report on the project, with an income and expenditure account showing how the finance was being handled, and how the mortgage loan was going down week by week and month by month. Then came the time when the mortgage was paid off, and the property became wholly theirs – and they could use the deeds as a deposit to acquire another property. They all became very interested in this because it was *their* money, and they could see for themselves how money could multiply, and they could learn the wisdom of prudence – none of my boys has grown up to be a fool with money."

And then there was their religious life. All those family dinners started with prayers, and the boys were all told of the work their father did as a Bishop.

"The Mormon church is divided into wards," Mr. Osmond explained. "Each ward has around 800 people and its own chapel, and then five or six wards together make what we call a Stake ... the wards are like large families, each with a Bishop and two counsellors – and it was our job to take care of the immediate needs of the families in the ward by looking after those in need, by mutual improvement schemes, and by training young people.

"Virl and Tommy both became Eagle Scouts, and then later went on missions for the Church in Canada. Then Alan and Wayne both became Star Scouts in groups affiliated to the Church, and if they hadn't been in music they would probably have become missionaries, too, maybe going to another country, mingling with other people, and spreading the work of the Church ... but since they started working in music, we have always taken the view that they are fulfilling their duty to the Church in the work they do, and in the way they are seen to uphold the standards. As a family, we give ten per cent of everything we earn back to the Church."

CHAPTER THREE

Although they had given their children every opportunity to learn music and to play different instruments, the thought that this might be where their future careers lay had never entered the heads of George and Olive Osmond until one weekend when they decided to go on a family outing to the Yellowstone national park.

Until that landmark day, the Osmonds had lived through a very normal childhood – made different only by the exceptional care their parents took to ensure that the boys all developed their individual talents. It was something very important to Mrs. Osmond particularly, who though she had been working as a secretary when first she married and had sung in the evenings with a dance band as well as playing saxophone came from a long line of teachers, from a family who regarded education as an end in itself.

On the two occasions when I had long, detailed discussions with Mr. and Mrs. Osmond on their remarkable family, they told me many anecdotes illustrating the way in which they had both worked so hard to bring up their children not only within the traditions of their Church but also to respect other people, to be sensible with money, to work hard, and to find learning a pleasure. At the same time, they were careful not to make all this appear unnatural – either within the family or to others. It was to be a way of life, not something that the seven sons did against their will.

Before they went into television, the Osmonds went

to a State-run school in Ogden, Utah, just like the children of any other local family. The school, named after President Abraham Lincoln, had around 800 pupils then, though its buildings have since been demolished. But it was those family schoolrooms at home that made so much difference.

"On the walls, I always used to have the alphabet in different forms – so that they would start learning how to assemble words when they were very young . . . in our first house, the school room was in the attic – but we had three houses after that," Mrs. Osmond told me. "Each one had its own schoolroom. We had this theory that if you create interesting surroundings for children in their home, this is going to improve their attitude to learning. This was the reason we always had musical instruments available so that they could pick them up and play with them as and when they wanted to . . . they could learn to play bass or guitar, pick up a trombone, or sit down at the piano or organ and try to play that.

"The important thing to us was that it was what *they* wanted to do ... we provided the equipment, the instruments, leaving them to discover the different things they could do with them. At that time, we were in the real estate business so Father was able to buy bigger houses as the family grew, and they grew up so differently.

"Wayne always had this deep interest in mathematics, so we bought him all the books we could find on mathematics ... even when he was a little boy, Donny was always keen on anything mechanical. I remember once he asked his father if he could have the old tin box in which he kept his razor. George gave it to him, and Donny went away, pleased as he could be – and came back later, having turned it into a telephone, and he was very young at that time, much younger than you would expect for a boy to do something like that, no more than six or seven.

"They were all keen on sports, too. It wasn't just studious things that caught their imagination. Wherever the boys were, you would soon find a football . . . they loved body surfing if ever we went to the coast . . . sometimes, they would go off on a weekend hike and go fishing. Later, when we bought the ranch at Wartske, we would all go down to stay there as a family, and the boys would go riding up into the hills, where they would make fires and have their own cook-outs . . . and if they went down to the lake, swimming or boating or water-skiing there would always be water fights, always fun and games when they were in the water together. Life was never too serious – though if one of them said he wanted to follow up a special interest, we would encourage it . . . we arranged a correspondence course on English Literature for Jay, buying him the books he needed to follow this through, and then later he and Wayne both took up mechanical courses."

"I never allowed any of my children to get out of line," said Mr. Osmond, who believes that all children respect parents who impose discipline in the home, and combine this with firm guidance. "You have to give them guidance when they are young so that this becomes a habit when they are older . . . you put them on a course for life. I have always been a very strict father – you have to be with nine children . . . and they have all had a spanking if they have needed it . . . we always had a saying in the house, "Father is not always right, but he is always Father."

"We always followed the principle that Olive would give them love, and I would give them discipline – and we gave them that discipline without any inhibition of their minds. Donny never gave me any trouble. None of them did. I never allowed them to step out of line, but I always encouraged them to project themselves."

Mr. Osmond further explained the importance he attached to giving this guidance within the framework of their religion. "Unless you do that, a child is going to create habits that are really not necessary to him . . . that is why we attach so much importance in the Mormon church to missionary work, because we believe this encourages young people to understand their beliefs in relation to the world as a whole.

"The boys were all brought up expecting to spend two years of their lives after leaving school in missionary work – and that was exactly what Virl and Tommy did. They both spent two years in Canada as missionaries, which was very good for them both, teaching them a lot about their religion, and about life, and as a family this brought us even closer together, because we shared everything that Virl and Tommy did, reading through their letters together on Friday evenings so that their younger brothers grew up knowing that they may be doing the same work one day – which they may still be yet for all we know.

"We also taught them that to squander was very wrong, and that was why those family money lessons were so important. They brought the realities of finance home to the boys. For that first project, we borrowed 1,000 dollars at six per cent interest, and then we used that to build on towards the next project, and as a family we watched that project grow, making all the decisions together. Now, all my sons are good businessmen. They all work hard, and are very cautious with their money."

So here were the pillars on which the Osmonds' family life was built – religious worship, discipline, giving money to their church, being prudent in their finances, self-sufficient in their home so far as they could be, and always with a constant quest for knowledge.

"All the boys were interested in archaeology, so when we came to London the first time we all went down to see the Tutenkhamun exhibition together. Archaeology is another important aspect of our Faith because we believe that Jesus Christ visited America, and that is what the message in the Book of Mormon is all about – that there is evidence for people to believe that Christianity was established in America before the tribal Indian civilisations developed.

"There was a civilisation in central America that we are especially interested in because no scientists have been able to say who these people were, though they had considerable knowledge, working with a numeral system with fifteen digits instead of ten, and had developed an accurate calendar ... they knew how to transfer blocks in building, understood the principles of construction and were evidently a highly advanced people – because it appears that they knew all this four hundred years ahead of the Pharoahs."

Now, to encourage their children to further their studies if they wish (possibly taking sabbaticals from their work in the music business), Mr. and Mrs. Osmond have one of their homes actually on the campus of the Brigham Young University at Provo in Utah. "There's a quite different atmosphere there," says Mrs. Osmond. "You never find a crowd of young girls outside the door because it's a university. You never get the screaming type."

The building was formerly a three-storey office block,

with each floor 3,000 sq. ft. in size. To the designs of their son Virl, who is a trained architect, the Osmond family have had the building gutted and then re-fitted as a family home. They moved in towards the end of 1972. Now, they have a music room and recording studio on the ground floor; offices for the Osmonds' various business enterprises on the first floor, and then their private living quarters on the second floor, overlooking the University quadrangle. Also stored away in the building are all the family records – tapes of every TV appearance they have ever made, film clips, photographs, all their press cuttings and record company press handouts, all neatly filed.

"In future, we will be able to take a year off if we want to – and the boys will be able to attend any course they want to at the University," said Mrs. Osmond, who still attaches the same importance that she has always done to their education, taking a tutor with her around the world for Jimmy, Marie and Donny, who all have lessons during the morning, no matter what part of the world they are visiting (since her marriage to Merrill, Mary has been tutoring Jimmy and Marie – she was already a qualified teacher before meeting Merrill).

All these horizons have opened to the Osmonds directly as a result of that car journey to Yellowstone National Park, which I mentioned in the first paragraph of this chapter. It was a journey that started off as a family picnic outing. They set off with a basket in the back of the car packed with food and fresh drinks so that they could all eat out in the park while they watched the herds of buffalo, the deer and the bears and other animals living in this natural environment.

On their way back to Ogden, Mr. Osmond sat at the

wheel, and started to sing a song that he remembered from childhood, "The Old Oaken Bucket". After he had sung a verse or two, he suggested that they all join in, and then that they sing different verses together in harmony.

"Suddenly, something seemed to happen," he told me, as he remembered that evening. "They started to sing real good . . . the harmonies were just right, and we moved on to other songs, singing out loud as we bowled along in the car. The Osmonds were born that night because they started singing in harmony just like that at our Friday evening family dinners because Olive and I asked them to."

The date that really stands out in Mrs. Osmond's memory of those early years is October 13th., 1959, because that was the day her first and only daughter Olive Marie was born – on George Osmond's birthday! (The night before Mrs. Osmond had had a dream that a doctor came to her bed, and said she would have a boy, James Arthur – which she did three and a half years later!)

That afternoon, the brothers all went along to the hospital, stood outside the window of the ward where Mrs. Osmond was resting, and started to sing in close harmony "I Want A Girl Just Like The Girl That Married Dear Old Dad".

"That was one of the most lovely memories I have of their childhood," she says.

By now, Mr. Osmond, a very proud father, was starting to tell his friends in the Ogden church community how well his sons sang together, and it wasn't long before he was asked if they would entertain elders of the church after a luncheon. That really started the ball rolling. After that they were in regular demand for

Mormon social functions in other parts of Utah as well as Ogden, sometimes travelling up to fifty miles a night – more for the fun than the money, because they seldom earned more than ten or twenty dollars. Then one day early in 1962 they were asked to go down to California to help with a Church crusade, singing at various functions.

Mr. Osmond decided to take the whole family, and when there was an afternoon free in their itinerary he gave the boys a special treat, something they had long been looking forward to, a day out at Disneyland.

There, they wandered between the massive rides, marvelling at the faithful, larger than life reconstructions of Wild West ghost towns, Indian battles, and charging buffalo, the Moon Ride, the Journey to the Centre of the Earth, Haunted Houses and Mississippi Steamboats – all as large as life and electronically operated so that the young Osmonds could step aboard and feel that time had stopped a hundred years before.

As they walked through the vast Disneyland estate, the family passed a restaurant where a barber shop quartet was singing in close harmony just the same style songs that they had sung that night on the way back from Yellowstone Park, at their Friday evening family parties, and at so many Mormon functions.

The boys stood at the back, started to sing themselves, moving their hands with a natural rhythm – and were invited up on the stage. Then, by one of those strange coincidences that so often shape the course of a star's career, just at that moment a Disney executive walked by, smiled when he saw them, stopped and was immediately impressed.

He introduced himself to Mr. Osmond, and suggested that the four boys (Donny was still very young) appear for a few nights on the stage themselves. This they did – and were then invited to appear on a Walt Disney TV special "Disneyland After Dark".

The show was repeated after the Osmonds had already returned home to Utah, and it was quite by chance that this repeat was seen by Andy Williams' father, Mr. Jay Williams, who knew that his son was looking for a group of young singers to appear with him on the TV show that he was shortly to begin recording.

Mr. Williams phoned the Disney TV studios, got Mr. Osmond's telephone number in Utah, and then phoned him himself, suggesting that the boys audition for his son – which they did. Andy included them in the very first show in 1962, and they afterwards appeared with him every week for four years, which soon persuaded Mr. and Mrs. Osmond to buy another home in California, which was where Jimmy was born on April 16th., 1963.

CHAPTER FOUR

California became the Osmonds' second home early in the Sixties when they started appearing weekly on Andy Williams' American TV series, which was also shown in Britain by BBC TV. Before that big break-through, their father had made many attempts to get his sons noticed outside Utah.

Once, their grandfather suggested they should make their own film and send it to the producers of all the major TV shows to show them all how good they were – and this they did. Again, in 1960, George drove the boys to Los Angeles hoping that they would be given an audition by the orchestra leader Lawrence Welk, but that didn't come off, either – though it must be remembered that the Osmonds were then very young, and their father was aiming very high indeed.

But they still carried on travelling to different towns in their home state, with George Osmond often driving them fifty miles and more a night so that they would earn barely enough to pay for the petrol. "We'd have just about enough left for an ice cream cone," said Alan, years later.

Then, the four boys – Alan, Wayne, Merrill and Jay – were still at the Lincoln county school, still rising early each morning to help Virl and Tommy with Daisy, to feed the chickens before going to school. "We always used to get up by 3 a.m. in the morning, specially in the summer when it was lighter," says Alan.

Donny was still just a toddler, but a very determined one – which is one of the main memories that his mother and father have of him at that time. "If he set his mind to do something, he would never give up," recalls Mr. Osmond. "The first time he went out on a sledge, he fell off – and climbed straight back on with his jaw set so hard . . . and it was the same with everything. Later, when we bought the ranch and our horses, Donny was the one who threw himself into it, becoming one of the better riders in the family . . . and the same with water skiing, with football, with surfing. He was always determined not to let his elder brothers leave him behind . . . and if there were fights or squabbles, then Donny would keep his end up."

When that big TV break-through came, Donny was still only just approaching his third birthday – and though he would join in when they sang around the table on Friday evenings, there was no question of his appearing on TV, too. Not at first!

But Mrs. Osmond, who was encouraging them all to learn music – starting with the saxophone, which was the instrument she used to play – made him an identical pair of trousers and a matching shirt, just like the ones she had cut out and stitched together on the family sewing machine for his elder brothers, always giving them dark coloured trousers with shirts in different shades.

At first, the family thought that the "Disneyland After Dark" TV special was just another false start. They filmed it, saw it on television, and then returned home to Ogden, the boys to their school, and father to his business interests in insurance and real estate. But, luckily for them, the show was repeated – and it was then that Jay Williams saw them, searched for their phone number, and contacted Mr. Osmond at home in Ogden, suggesting they audition for Andy's show. The family was delighted. They applied for an audition date – and then out came the car again for another drive down to California.

They passed the audition, were offered a contract – and Mr. Osmond, who had by now made enough money to be able to plan an early retirement, decided to sell his businesses, move to California with his whole family so that the boys could make the most of this opportunity – even though the eldest member of the group, Alan, was only thirteen years old with Wayne aged eleven, Merrill aged nine, and Jay, aged seven. From now on, school was out – instead they all had private tutors, working just as hard (and Merrill claims much harder!) than children of their own generation attending the State schools.

"We always spent the mornings working on school subjects if we were in the studios in the afternoon," says Merrill. "And we really had to work at it. There was no fooling around. It was hard work."

But not always so. Mr. and Mrs. Osmond never gave up that family home in Ogden, so whenever there was a break in the shooting schedule, back home they would all go – with Mr. Osmond determined to get closer and closer to his children.

"We got ourselves a cabin up in the hills of North Utah, about eighty miles from Ogden – and there we'd spend our summer holidays . . . the cabin was by a lake, and we'd go fishing and swimming . . . then some week-ends, I'd take the boys for long hikes, and we'd have our own cook-outs up in the hills, grilling hamburgers on open fires. They were all keen to be Boy Scouts, so we'd sit by the fire and learn how to tie knots, with Virl and Tommy always showing them the way because they'd already qualified as Eagle Scouts by this time.

"We really tried to do things together as a family, and at the same time the boys were all learning independence because this was quite a remote area with no sightseers, no-one to disturb them or ask for autographs, which was something we were beginning to need at weekends, too, because the pressure was starting to build up a little down at the studio . . . not too much, you know, but enough for me to feel that I should get them away at weekends."

Their act had become one of the most popular spots on the show – with Alan, Wayne, Merrill and Jay often standing shoulder to shoulder to sing, like the old style harmony-singing barber shop quartets. Viewers thought they looked cute. Each boy was a little taller than his immediate younger brother so there they would stand, side by side – and by the time he was four, young Donny would sometimes come on and sing with them, too, as Marie and Jimmy have in recent years when the Osmonds have been appearing in cabaret and in concert.

Andy Williams was so pleased that he signed them to a five year contract for his own label, Barnaby, which was distributed by Columbia. "Nothing ever happened to us musically," Alan was to say later. "It just wasn't the right situation for us at the time ... although we liked rock music at that time, we couldn't get people to believe that that was what we should be doing ... on the TV shows, we often used to sing old-style songs, standards, not the sort of songs that were getting into the charts."

Exactly what went wrong in those early days is not clear, but Alan did say in an interview published in the "Melody Maker" (November 4th., 1972) that "Nothing ever happened ... it wasn't the right situation and Andy's been real good to us. He gave us our start, but it's been mismanagement in the early stages and we were hurt a lot. That's all I want to say about it. It was a growing thing ... we got on the Andy Williams show, and we were doing all these show business things and we were digging the rock scene, and we wanted to make a move ... it got to the point where we had to make a decision about going out on our own. We talked to Andy about it and told him. He once told us a long time ago, 'One of these days you're going to leave me like I left my brothers.' We said, 'No, Andy – never, never!' ... we left him. It's only natural. It's like when a person gets married or moves away from home. It's a growing period, and we took that step."

Through those growing years, the Osmonds – occasionally augmented by Donny – had appeared regularly on television. For four years, they were on the Andy Williams show weekly. In 1963, they also teamed up with actor Kurt Russell in another TV series, "The Travels of Jamie McPheeters". With Donny, still only five years old, they also appeared in their own TV special, "The Seven Little Foys", dancing as well as singing. When their four year run with Andy Williams ended, the brothers became regular guests on "The Jerry Lewis Show" – and sometimes appeared in cabaret or concert with artists like Nancy Sinatra, Phyllis Diller, Andy Williams and Pat Boone. They also toured Sweden and Japan (Jimmy had a No. 2 hit there in 1968 with a song called "My Little Darling", and was actually the first member of the family to get a gold disc – when he was five years old). Then in 1969, they rejoined Andy Williams for another year of weekly TV shows. But, as Alan said, the Osmonds were now itching to make records, having by now learned to play a wide range of musical instruments.

As well as lead guitar, Alan had now learned piano, saxophone, banjo and bass; Wayne could play tenor banjo, clarinet and flute, although on television he was usually only seen with either a saxophone or a rhythm guitar in his hands; Merrill's range of instruments included drums, bass guitar, trombone, saxophone and tenor banjo; even their drummer Jay could double on saxophone and banjo – while young Donny was proving a capable pianist and organist, and could also handle banjo, saxophone, bass and lead guitars. Their mother's tuition had proved invaluable; the Osmonds now needed no group, orchestra or backing musicians when they went into a recording studio – though in cabaret they would often use accompanists so that they could sing in close harmony and feature dance numbers.

"We'd always felt we were far more capable musically than people gave us credit for," Merrill told me.

Now, they were to prove it. They approached MGM Records and told the company's president, Mike Curb, that they would like to start recording – and eventually would like their own label (which has since been formed with the name Kolob, which Merrill told me was inspired by their religion – Kolob is the name given to what Mormons believe to be a governing planet at the heart of the Universe. They already have two protegees, a negro group they first heard in Baltimore at the recommendation of one of their security guards, Twins Plus Him, and the British trio Springfield Revival, who now record for Kolob, often using the Osmonds' own studio and frequently accompany them on American, British and European tours (see chapter seven).

The Osmonds were ready for this break-through in another way. After nine years of regular TV appearances, they felt more than prepared for live stage work – so

1971 saw them score three firsts, their first hit single in the States "One Bad Apple", which earned them a gold disc; their first headlining concert appearances, and their first solo TV special "The Osmond Brothers Show – He's My Brother". And the year also saw the emergence of Donny Osmond, firstly as a fulltime member of the group – bringing them up to five in number – and also as a solo singer, with his own solo hits when he was only twelve years old (with his voice still unbroken), rapidly becoming the top teenage draw in the States.

And they were ready in one other way, too – their parents had long since devoted their full time energies to their sons' career. Now, their life had become much more settled – with their main home in Ogden, with another one being planned in Provo, with that 2,300-acre ranch to retreat to up in the Utah hills, and another home in a western suburb of Los Angeles, Westwood.

"We've moved homes quite a few times with me being in real estate," Mr. Osmond told me. "When we first went out to live in California in 1962, I bought a Spanish-style house with a verandah with an acre of ground surrounding it with grapes, apricots and lemons growing there, and this small swimming pool ... it was a two-storey home, and we were very happy there – Donny especially because he's a very good swimmer ... the floors were slate rock. It was really nice."

But Mr. Osmond felt that this was not really the type of base they needed in Los Angeles since the family could get all the relaxation they needed returning home to Utah; what was wanted was a more functional building. So they bought a block of separate apartments – seven flats, which they linked together, giving them all the space they needed. It is close to the MGM offices and studios, and also to their own studios, which were recently completed with Donny (a keen student of electronics) supervising the installation of all the recording and mixing equipment.

Of all the places they have lived in, two have been most popular within the family – Ogden, because that was their family home with relatives nearby, and that cabin up in the mountains, which they called Hunsa after the last of the Tibetan mountain tribes, and because it was near a Utah mountain village called Huntsville. The Osmonds first acquired that home in 1960, before even their television career started – and right through the Sixties this was their hidden retreat, as it still is today, with very few people outside the family ever being invited there.

"In winter there, the temperature can drop to twenty degrees below zero," Mr. Osmond told me. "It gets real cold, but great fun . . . because there's thick snow on the ground, and the lakes are frozen over . . . in the early years, the boys used to go ice skating over the lakes, snow balling, and sliding down the slopes on their toboggans, and then we'd all run inside the cabin and have bowls of hot soup, which we always called our own special Hunsa Stew . . . then in the evenings, there'd be a log fire, and we'd all sit round the fire together.

"Because we started staying there long before the television thing started, the local people accept us. There's just this little village in the mountains with one little store – just like you see in some of the old Western films – where you can go in and buy food or candies, linen, saddles, lengths of cloth, hardware, plumping equipment, ropes and haulage tackle, cans of gas, anything you want. It's the sort of store that provides everything for the local people because they have nowhere else to go if they wanted to. As soon as we get back to Hunsa in the winter, the first thing the boys always used to want to do would be to go down to the store to see the people there, and make sure nothing had changed.

"All the boys ski, and they're very good, taking great care – which is just as well because one broken ankle could put us all out of business for months!

"They all love ice skating, and just tramping through the snow on snow shoes – which can be a great adventure just on its own because sometimes the snow is two and a half feet deep. Now, we've got snowmobiles up there so we can all go riding about on the snow, and that's a great attraction, I can tell you."

In a sense, all this was to prove the perfect safety valve – because 1971 saw them suddenly break out in the States, selling even more records that year than the Beatles had in any of their years together.

Their break-through was not overnight. The Osmonds had been gradually developing a teenage following before Mike Curb signed them to the MGM label. The second Andy Williams TV series – with Donny appearing every week with his brothers now – had brought them widespread coverage in the teenage magazines, especially for Donny, who was now twelve years old and the big teen attraction. In March, 1970, the family went back to Japan (they have now toured there four times) to appear at Expo 70 – and then when they returned to the States, Mike Curb signed them to the MGM label.

The first Osmond single to be released was a group one, "One Bad Apple", which they recorded down at the Muscle Shoals studios in Alabama, which had a reputation at the time for being *THE* studio. In December, 1970, the single became a hit – and spent six weeks at No. 1 in the U.S. charts. That same month, the Osmonds taped their first TV special "The Osmond Brothers Show – He's My Brother", which reached third slot in that week's audience ratings. But the family were not able to get back to Utah for the holiday season – for five years they had not been able to spend Christmas at home. Instead, they went back to Japan for another series of personal appearances – and spent Christmas Day itself at the Tokyo Hilton.

"We bought ourselves a small Christmas tree in a nearby park – a real Christmas tree, though not as big as the ones we grow ourselves back home in Utah," said Mr. Osmond. "Then we took it back to the hotel, stood around the tree and sang carols, feeling a little bit lonely, so far away from home."

They returned to the States to find that the group – and Donny – were both becoming very BIG indeed. The Osmonds' first album, titled just "Osmonds", had been released – and radio stations were being bombarded with requests from Donny fans asking for one track to be played again and again. The number was "Sweet And Innocent". MGM decided to take the track from the LP and release it as Donny's first solo single – and that, too, became a million-seller. By now, it was hard to find a teenage magazine in the States that did not feature Donny Osmond regularly on its cover – and spread over several pages inside.

In May, 1971, the Osmonds appeared on a concert stage for the very first time – until then their only live appearances had been as a supporting attraction in cabaret at Las Vegas to established stars like Nancy Sinatra, Andy Williams, Pat Boone and Petula Clark. But now their parents, their manager Ed Leffler and Mike Curb all thought the time had come for all those years of musical training to be put to the test – which it was for the very first time at Cleveland, Ohio, on May 28th., 1971. The next night, they performed again – this time in Columbus, Ohio, with a third concert at Houston, Texas, on May 30th. The stage shows were a big success with the largely teenage audiences – but even more important they gave the Osmonds themselves the confidence to agree plans for a coast-to-coast tour of the United States, which began in July, took them through 48 American cities, finishing early in September.

That year, the Osmonds sold more records in twelve months than any group had ever done – releasing three singles "One Bad Apple"/"He Ain't Heavy He's My Brother" (which earned them a gold disc and then a platinum record for sales worth over 2,000,000 U.S. dollars), "Double Loving"/"Chilly Winds" (not a big hit), and then "Yo-Yo"/"Keep On My Side" (gold disc for sales over 1,000,000 dollars). They also had three albums that year that earned gold discs – "The Osmonds", "Home Made" and "Phase III". And then 1971 also saw Donny Osmond emerging just as strongly on his own – he had three million-selling singles "Sweet And Innocent"/"Flirtin' ", "Go Away Little Girl"/"Time To Ride" and "Hey Girl"/"I Knew You When" *plus* two million-selling LPs "The Donny Osmond Album" and "To You With Love, Donny". Between them that year, the Osmond family grossed well over 12,000,000 U.S. dollars just in record sales.

But their parents were very anxious that this sudden rise to stardom, with all the security problems that went with it, should not damage their life together as a family. George and Olive Osmond decided to travel everywhere with their sons – taking Jimmy and Marie along, too, together with a tutor so that every day school lessons would continue normally, no matter where they might be. And their parents also insisted that, hard though the Osmonds were all keen to work, their schedule should be organised in such a way that each period of intensive travelling, concerts and recording should be followed by a break, giving them the chance to relax back home in Utah.

In June, after those first concerts in Ohio and Texas, the boys went back to the family ranch, and spent a month riding horses, water-skiing, fishing, swimming – sometimes helping the ranch hands to round up cattle. And then again in September, when the tour finished, it was back to Utah for another rest before they started recording again – and it was when they returned to Los Angeles for those sessions that disaster almost struck the family.

As always, Donny had gone to bed on the night of September 24th., 1971, around 10 p.m. (Their parents had always insisted on early nights as well as a regular diet to keep them all fit for their heavy schedule of work). As he lay in bed, Donny felt a violent pain in his stomach. A doctor was called, and he asked: "Have you been eating anything that might have upset you?"

"Only peanuts," said Donny, managing a smile.

At first, the doctor thought the trouble might be indigestion – and he advised against any more peanuts for the time being. But it was more serious than that. The pain got worse, and during the night Donny slipped out of bed and went to his parents' room. By now, he was shaky on his feet, feverish, sweating one moment, feeling cold the next, with his eyes red and strained. As he knocked on his parents' door, he said: "I think we'd better call the doctor again."

This time, he was rushed into the Beverley Glen Hospital where specialists advised an immediate operation. It was acute appendicitis, and his appendix had swollen so much that it was now close to bursting, which could have been fatal.

At first his parents hesitated, but Donny insisted that the operation should go ahead – and he remembers very little after that because he soon slipped into unconsciousness. "It was one of the toughest moments of our lives," his father said afterwards. "We were all very worried, and we prayed that night for Donny . . . but he wasn't too worried himself, though he was in great pain. "I'll be all right," he told us."

As the year ended, MGM Records revealed that astonishing rate of record sales – the 12,000,000 dollars was quite apart from their tours and TV shows, their cabaret and songwriting, their merchandising income, and their overseas royalties. Christmas that year was again spent away from their Utah home – this time down in Florida, where the Osmond family had been booked into the Diplomatic Hotel in Miami, where the brothers were appearing nightly in cabaret.

By now, Donny was such a major teenage attraction that he was trapped in his hotel. Though the sun was shining (a great change from all those knee-deep snowy Christmases at Hunsa), he could seldom get out to enjoy it. Swimming in the sea or bathing on the beach was out of the question – though he could walk along the beach late at night with his father, talking excitedly about the next big date in the Osmond family diary, their first trip to Britain. "Perhaps we'll meet the Queen," said Donny.

Originally their manager Ed Leffler and recording company MGM had been discussing plans to bring the Osmonds to London in January, 1972, but these arrangements had to be cancelled when Wayne developed a hernia – he thinks he probably strained himself playing football – and he had to go into hospital for a minor operation. Their first trip to Britain was then rescheduled for May, 1972 – and as soon as this became known the Osmonds were invited to appear in a special Royal Gala at the London Palladium, which was being staged by ATV to raise funds for the British Olympic Team Appeal Fund, and which the Queen and the Duke of Edinburgh had agreed to attend.

In Britain, Polydor – the record company that distributes MGM's product – quickly arranged a press conference for the day the Osmonds arrived, laying on three Rolls Royces to take the family direct from Heathrow Airport, where they were due to arrive at 10.15 a.m. to the Churchill Hotel, where the press conference was scheduled for 12 noon with a photo call at 2.30 p.m.

So far the Osmonds had never had a hit record in Britain, but Polydor were in no doubt as to the importance of the visit. They issued invitations to the press, telling them:

> *THE OSMONDS*
>
> The six Osmond Brothers Alan (23), Wayne (20), Merrill (19), Jay (17), Donny (15) and Little Jimmy (8) are America's hottest musical property bar none. They have gained eleven Gold Discs in the last ten months, beating the Beatles and every previous record holder. Their concerts are a sell-out everywhere. This is their first-ever British visit, which, apart from the ATV show will take in three more TV shows."

But the British press were unimpressed. Polydor had laid out rows and rows of gold-edged chairs seated in red velvet for the press conference, and arranged a table with a battery of microphones on a raised dais for the Osmonds to answer questions from the audience. But hardly any journalists turned up. There was only a handful of people there, including myself. After delaying the press conference for nearly half an hour with statements that The Osmonds had been delayed and that the plane had been late, and their cars had been held up (all the time with anxious glances at the door to see if any more pressmen were on their way), the formal conference was finally cancelled, and instead the few of us who were there were invited into an adjoining room where we sat and chatted with the Osmond of our choice, quietly in groups of two and three people, for nearly an hour and a half.

On May 22nd, The Osmonds taped their show at the London Palladium – and managed to avoid people in the audience realising that Donny's microphone had gone dead. Wayne hurriedly switched mikes when it was Donny's turn to sing. "I don't think anyone out there noticed – but that made us feel nervy," said Donny afterwards.

Afterwards, the Osmonds had to go back to their dressing room and change into evening dress so that they could line up with Marie, Jimmy and their parents to meet the Queen and the Duke of Edinburgh.

"That will always be one of the proudest moments of our life," says Donny. "She really is a lovely lady . . . when she came up to me and put out her hand, I bowed and said: 'It's really nice to meet you, M'am' . . . she thanked me, and then she turned to Jimmy and said, 'You did a very good job' . . . The Queen asked Wayne all about the family and how many brothers and sisters we had, and he told her all about Tommy's wedding."

By now, The Queen and the Duke of Edinburgh had

spent more time talking to the Osmond family than most of the other people in the show, and the officials seemed a little worried that the pre-arranged timetable would not be kept. The Queen noticed their anxiety, and told one official: "I want to have a longer talk with these boys."

And she did – asking Marie and Merrill about the problems of having to keep up to date with their education with such a busy schedule of concerts and recording sessions, and having a long chat afterwards with Mr. and Mrs. Osmond, telling them what a fine family they had. "That was a real honour for us, meeting the Queen and Duke like that – and they were so nice and friendly," Mrs. Osmond told me afterwards.

CHAPTER FIVE

The Osmond family's first trip to Britain in May 1972, had immediate effect. The group's single "Down By The Lazy River" soon became their first chart entry – and then after their return to the States, Donny had his first solo hit, "Puppy Love", which went to No. 1 in the charts in July. Then he had another major hit, "Too Young". This was to prove the start of what the press were quick to call Osmondmania, but it had only started to snowball after their return home to Utah; their actual stay in London was peace itself compared with what was to happen when they returned later in the year.

After that show at the London Palladium, the family celebrated with dinner at a Chelsea restaurant, and then Donny, Jimmy and Marie went back to the Churchill hotel with their parents while their elder brothers decided to take a look at the London clubs, the Speakeasy and Tramps – where it created quite a stir to see musicians who were happy with just a glass of orange juice.

The family also visited the tourist spots – Buckingham Palace, Big Ben, the Houses of Parliament and Trafalgar Square; played football in Hyde Park; went boating on the Serpentine (which produced a good selection of promotional photos for Polydor), and shopping in Carnaby Street and the Kings Road. For Donny, the keen studio engineer of the group, the big excitement of that trip was being invited down to the AIR London studios by one of the directors, George Martin, who had been the Beatles' recording manager.

"I wish we'd been able to get around more," Merrill told me afterwards. "We only had two days for sight-seeing and going round the shops – but this was quite something for us, to have two days in which we could walk around a city, just looking around. It was marvellous to be able to see so much because usually when we go to a place for the first time, we have to stay most of the time in our hotels because of the security problems. It's become the custom now to book us into hotels with a whole floor to ourselves – so that security guards can stand by the staircases and the lift shafts and seal off the whole floor. That's what always happens when we're touring in the States."

Alan agreed that this had become quite a problem for them, with Utah now the only place where they could walk about normally without being pursued by fans.

"It's very difficult to go to the front of the stage because they try to grab you," said Alan. "You have to learn not to answer knocks on the door because you don't know whether a whole lot of them have broken through the security system, which they still manage to do sometimes. When we're in hotels, we can never use elevators or staircases – which seems very strange to our friends when they come to visit us. Often when we're on a stage back home, there'll be as many as thirty policemen standing at the back of the stage, but still they manage to get through, and make a grab at you.

"When we were appearing in cabaret in Florida last Christmas, we couldn't leave the hotel during the day because of the girls crowding outside . . . and one group of girls even got up to a room on the sixth or seventh floor above us and started to lower themselves down to our floor on a rope . . . the first we knew of it was when we glanced towards the windows, and suddenly saw these ropes hang down, and dangle outside.... I went over to the window and looked up there, and there they were, so I went out to see them, and talked them out of it, and agreed that we'd see them in the hallway if they took back the ropes.... I was worried that they might kill themselves."

The Osmonds had been expecting the same sort of problems in London that May. But instead, they could move around the London streets on foot – though Merrill told me they were still recognised. "Some girls recognised us and this was a bit overwhelming, just walking down the street – but that never offends us," said Merrill, who is, like his brothers, a natural diplomat. "We are fond of them. We are lucky to have so many fans, and when that first group of girls came up to me and said they knew I was Merrill, I told them, 'I thought you wouldn't recognise me.' And they said they had seen us on television."

It was to be a very different story later in the year when Merrill and his family returned to London for their second visit. After the success of "Down By The Lazy River" and then Donny's two smash singles "Puppy Love" and "Too Young", Polydor thought the timing was right to bring the Osmonds back to London again – and one of their top executives, Roger Holt, was sent to Las Vegas on September 28th to spend a week with the Osmond family, discussing plans for another trip to London, which was being tentatively planned for the end of October.

"I'd never been to Las Vegas before, and found Caesar's Palace quite amazing," Holt told me. "It was just like a Roman palace, with statues and pillars and thick pile carpets – and fruit machines wherever you looked.

"The town is always full of gamblers, so the hotels put

on these big star shows with people like Frank Sinatra, Tom Jones, Engelbert Humperdinck and the Osmonds so that the wives and children have somewhere to go in the evenings while their menfolk are all out gambling . . . the whole town is built to encourage people to spend money, and to make them happy at the same time . . . and that's why groups like the Osmonds are booked in there."

Roger Holt spent nearly a week in Las Vegas discussing the organisation of the next trip – the publicity arrangements, the question of work permits (which were arranged by their agents for the trip, Management, Agency and Music), the venues at which they would appear in concert, the group's requirements for stage lighting, sound and amplification, the TV shows they might do, and the number of security guards that would be required day and night at their hotel (because Polydor had already realised that this trip would be very different to the last one).

There was also the question of which records to release – because "Crazy Horses" was already a hit in the States (and they had an album completed with the same title). A live album had also been recorded, and Donny had already had three solo albums issued in the States – where each one had grossed over 1,000,000 U.S. dollars in sales. And then there was Jimmy, who had already recorded "Long Haired Lover From Liverpool" – which had not been released anywhere yet, although he had become so successful in Japan.

"There was a lot to discuss," said Holt. "At first, I wasn't going to release 'Crazy Horses' because people only knew Donny's singles 'Puppy Love' and 'Too Young'. . . . 'Crazy Horses' was a very different type of song which they had written and arranged themselves, a much heavier style of music – very different to the sort of image that people were starting to build up here of the Osmonds, and I was afraid that people wouldn't accept a drastic change in style. . . . I thought 'Crazy Horses' was perhaps too heavy for this market, and that was why I'd issued 'Puppy Love' first of all . . . then I thought I'd bring out 'Hey Girl' (which had already been a million-seller for Donny in the States) . . . but I saw them on TV and became very enthusiastic about the Osmonds, and changed my mind, realising it would be a mistake to hold back 'Crazy Horses', which I'd got to like even more myself, and I thought, 'Why not let more people know they're so talented'."

Roger Holt also saw the Osmonds several nights at Caesar's Palace, where they had a totally different stage act to the one used for concert tours – with costumes designed by Bill Bellew, who had also produced stage costumes for Elvis Presley's cabaret appearances, and with carefully orchestrated dance numbers.

"I was very, very impressed – because they were putting on a show that was quite different to the style of show I had seen them do on television," said Holt. "I thought they were so talented. I just couldn't believe it when I saw that cabaret show. It was a lot different from what I'd seen them do before, a show that older people would enjoy as well, with songs I hadn't heard them sing before, and the whole production was so totally professional."

By now, Roger Holt had decided – and the Osmonds had agreed – that the bold approach to their London trip was the one to take. Instead of just following up Donny's two hits with another of his already successful American releases, Polydor and MGM agreed to attack the British market on all fronts – with The Osmonds releasing "Crazy Horses", with Jimmy releasing "Long Haired

Lover From Liverpool", and Donny bringing out "Why" all on the same day. And for a while there were even tentative plans to make the attack even broader than that with another single, this time from Marie – but that idea was postponed. And with the Christmas season on its way, they all agreed to release a good range of Christmas stocking fillers as well.

With the plans now agreed for the Osmonds to arrive in Britain at the end of October, MGM and Polydor now had the most extraordinary range of albums and singles either in stock, in the shops or being produced down at their pressing plant. The date of release for those three singles was set for November 3rd, and by then Polydor was able to tell the press that all these recordings were now available:

THE OSMONDS

Three singles – "Sweet and Innocent"/"Motown Special", "Hold Her Tight"/"Love Is" and "Crazy Horses"/"That's My Gal".

Three albums – "Phase III", "The Osmonds Live" and "Crazy Horses" (which was timed to reach the shops in January).

DONNY OSMOND

Five singles – "Go Away Little Girl"/"Time To Ride", "Hey Girl"/"I Knew You When", "Puppy Love"/"Let My People Go", "Too Young"/"Love Me" and "Why"/"Lonely Boy".

Three albums – "The Donny Osmond Album", "Portrait of Donny" and "Too Young" (timed for release in December).

JIMMY OSMOND

One single – "Long Haired Lover From Liverpool"/ "Mother of Mine".

Never before in pop music had one family released so much at one time. The stage was now set for an enormous publicity build-up – helped by announcements on Radio Luxembourg of the time of arrival of the Osmonds' plane at London Airport, and the release to the press of the fact that the group would be staying at the Churchill Hotel.

Polydor helped to fuel the fans' ardour, announcing that free albums would be given to the first fans who bought tickets for the Osmonds' debut concert at the Rainbow – over a hundred fans slept out overnight at the Rainbow the night before the box office opened! Manager Ted Way said: "I have been involved in Beatles concerts, but demand for the Osmonds' concerts far exceeds anything I have ever experienced in over ten years of theatre management."

Polydor also announced that fans could hear latest details of the Osmond's plans if they phoned 01-499 6241 where there was a 24-hours-a-day message service. Later Polydor said in one of their press releases that this "has resulted in chaos on the 499 London area exchange (full details of this can be obtained from Mr. I. R. McIntyre, GPO Senior Telecommunications Superintendent at 437 8060 ext 440)".

Throughout the week preceding the Osmonds' arrival, there was a half-hourly show on Radio Luxembourg reminding fans that the Osmonds were due to arrive at London Airport at 10.30 a.m. on Sunday, October 29th. Their flight, TW760, would come to Terminal Three, said the radio reports, and then the Osmonds would be driven to Terminal Two so that any fans waiting there could see them.

In those half-hourly shows – aired every night at 8.30 p.m. from Monday, October 23rd to Friday, October 27th, there were interviews with The Osmonds; their records were played, and details of their trip were constantly repeated.

It was a quite blatant attempt to build up the fans' expectancy before the group arrived – but even so touch-down at London Airport came as quite a shock for the Polydor staff waiting there to meet the Osmonds off the plane. There were thousands of girls running hysterical around the airport, screaming, shouting, the tension building up all the time as first the Jackson Five arrived on one plane, and then Elton John arrived ... and then THE OSMONDS.

The spivs were cleaning up, selling hundreds of Donny and Osmonds posters. Girls were running in all directions waving scarves and banners with the words DONNY and OSMONDS plastered across their backs, their pants and their posters. Some papers said next morning that there were 8,000 girls there. Others said 10,000 and 12,000. All were agreed that the scenes had been wildly chaotic.

And for the Osmonds, it couldn't have happened on a better day. Sunday is the day when Fleet Street needs news most because most organisations that usually supply it are shut down for the weekend. There is little happening politically or in sport or in entertainment. So next day, the arrival of the Osmonds was plastered over the centre pages of most national papers. Osmondmania had arrived – and because the fans were so much younger than any that had followed The Beatles or The Rolling Stones, they, too, were given new names – THE

WEENYBOPPERS or THE WEENIES. The music press were near ecstasy. Next week, "Disc and Music Echo" had their centre spread of the airport scenes with the headline, "A HYSTERICAL, HISTORICAL DAY WHEN POP CAME BACK TO MUSIC". Both the "Melody Maker" and "New Musical Express" called it the "BATTLE OF THE BOPPERS", and the "Melody Maker" had another feature entitled, "WHO SAID IT COULDN'T HAPPEN AGAIN?"

Reporter Mike Ledgerwood told the readers of "Disc and Music Echo":

> "The rock clock went back almost ten years as fan fever turned the full cycle . . . pop music entered another era of hysteria. The return of the teeny idol is here. A new generation of fans has now arrived . . . the SCREAMAGERS! And they're giving the music scene a much-needed tonic.
>
> "It really was like Beatlemania all over again! Fan hysteria on a scale unmatched in nearly a decade erupted in London last weekend when both the Osmond Brothers and the Jackson Five jetted in within a few hours of each other.
>
> "Scenes of wild excitement at Heathrow Airport – where hundreds of girls had spent the night – greeted their arrival. It was astonishing."

Together with other reporters, Ledgerwood had been at the airport since early morning and had seen the arrival of the Jackson Five when hundreds of girls stormed forward, sweeping policemen off their feet and doing over £500 damage to the Rolls-Royce hired to take them to their hotel (also the Churchill). Afterwards, the airport almost returned to normal – but thousands of girls were arriving now on foot, by bus, by coach and by car – and there were regular announcements over the airport's public address system that the Queens Building, overlooking the runway, would be opened at 8.30 a.m. when fans could go up to see the group's plane arrive. Ledgerwood reported:

> "The scenes were quite extraordinary, frightening; amazingly reminiscent of the Beatlemania era, in fact . . . the Queens Building was bulging with fervent fans eager for just a brief glimpse of darling Donny. And the whole atmosphere exploded like Guy Fawkes night . . ."

In the "Melody Maker", Richard Williams reported that by the time the Osmonds arrived at the airport, touched down and were driven to the front of the Queens Building where their fans could see them,

> ". . . there were fans dripping off several layers of the roof, clutching banners distributed by the record company, who had shrewdly commandeered the public address system and were playing the 'Portrait of Donny' album over it . . . and (when screams greeted Donny's arrival) the volume, I swear, drowned the sound of an accelerating Boeing as the Famous Family debouches from its TWA bus and makes for a pair of Rolls Phantoms idling quietly on the tarmac.
>
> "There's Alan and Jay and Merrill and Wayne and Jimmy and DONNY! Donny, every inch the star, smiling that sweet Pepsodent smile and waving languidly to girls who're just about going beserk with love.
>
> "I hate to say it, but Jay and Merrill and Wayne might just as well not have bothered to make the trip.

"Alan's the older girls' dreamboat, Donny is everybody's sweetheart, and tiny Jimmy, nine years old, attracts, – would you believe – the maternal instinct in girls who aren't even . . . well, *you* know . . . yet.

"And right behind them, with benign smiles of Mormon happiness lighting their faces are Mr. and Mrs. Osmond, who can fairly be said to have created the whole shebang."

From the airport, the whole family were driven into central London to stay at the Churchill Hotel where another group of journalists, including myself, were waiting to meet them in a suite called The Library, apparently because it had rows of imitation book spines as its wallpaper. "Gosh, I hadn't expected a welcome quite like this," said Merrill as we sat talking, with the screams of around 2,000 girls echoing from outside in the street. "It wasn't like this last time we came."

The excitement stayed at fever pitch throughout the Osmonds' stay at the Churchill Hotel, with many girls playing truant from school to join the crowd that was always several hundred strong and sometimes ran into the thousands outside in Portman Square and the streets adjoining the Churchill, where they could look up at the bedroom windows where they already knew Donny and his brothers were relaxing behind lace curtains.

Sometimes, the crowd even turned vicious. One Polydor press officer was chased down the street because he was foolish enough to say "Yes" when asked if he had seen the Osmonds. He managed to jump into a taxi before being assaulted by the crowd of girls who were in fast pursuit, apparently believing that to touch someone who had himself touched an Osmond was the next best thing to actually meeting Donny himself! Three other girls attacked one of the policemen guarding the entrance to the Churchill Hotel. They had been trying to stop the Osmonds' cars leaving the hotel, and when the policeman stepped forward to clear a way through the crowd he was kicked and punched. The three girls, two aged 17 and one 16, were taken to Court and fined for assault. "It does not help matters when vicious little girls like you attack police officers and put them in hospital," said the Marylebone magistrate Mr. Kenneth Harington.

Roger Holt himself had not expected the chaos that erupted at the airport and outside the Churchill Hotel. "As soon as I saw those scenes at the airport, I had to lay on much greater security," he told me. "We had asked people not to say which hotel the Osmonds were staying at, but someone slipped up . . . the name of the hotel was given on the radio."

This happened by accident, Tony Prince, a Radio Luxembourg disc jockey, had been giving fans regular bulletins on the Osmonds' plans – and Holt sent him a copy of their detailed itinerary, which gave their arrival time at Heathrow, and an hour-by-hour schedule of their visits to TV studios, concerts, rehearsals, etc., throughout their stay in Britain. The name of the hotel was not on the sheet, but Prince mentioned that it was the Churchill.

"I phoned him up afterwards," Holt told me. "And I said to him, 'Why say that?' And he told me, 'No-one had told me not to!' So, in a sense, I suppose it was my fault, but none of us had expected the scenes that broke out.

"As soon as I saw those crowds at the airport, I got on the phone and hired a firm of security guards who provided security 24 hours a day for the Osmonds while they were here, sleeping in shifts in rooms adjoining theirs at the hotel . . . just at the Churchill Hotel alone, where the management were very co-operative, I had fifteen security guards on duty, and then I had another forty on duty at the Rainbow when the Osmonds gave their first concert.

"Getting them in and out of the hotel became such a problem that I arranged with the management to use the tradesmen's lift down into the garage in the basement, where they could get into their car . . . then we would have one car driven out one way as a decoy with people bunched down on the back seat with blankets over their heads, before the Osmonds themselves left in their Rolls . . . but the fans soon rumbled that ploy . . . they are very quick to see through any tricks of that sort.

"This was becoming so difficult for us, for the boys and the police, that the Police set up their own operations room nearby, with patrols all round the hotel. At one stage there was talk of hotel staff using a hose to get the kids out of the way so that the Osmonds' car could get through – but I stopped them doing that . . . after all, whatever nuisance they were causing, these were still the Osmonds' fans, the people who bought their records, and one had to remember that."

When the fans discovered the secret escape route, several hundred tried to force their way into the basement of the hotel – and there were dozens more clambering up fire escapes and trying to find ways of penetrating the building. Once when the Osmonds returned to their hotel and saw a crowd of girls waiting, they jumped out of their car in the basement, ran to the tradesmen's lift – and couldn't get the doors open. In the melee that followed, fans ripped Alan's shirt from his back, tore at Donny's hair and scratched his neck.

"The sad thing is that none of those girls really mean to hurt us," said Donny afterwards. "They are just ordinary fans, who would be quite normal if we met them on their own ... but when they get together in such great numbers, they start pushing and shoving, and if we didn't have these security guards, someone would get very seriously injured ... having security like this is as much for their protection as it is for ours."

When Holt went with Donny to the BBC studios in Portland Place, where he was interviewed by Ed Stewart on the Radio One programme "Junior Choice", there were hundreds more girls waiting in the street.

"We laid on another diversion car to get him away, but though this fooled some of them, many of the girls just carried on waiting outside the door ... when we left they surged forward, ripping Donny's jacket, and pulling at his hair.... I lifted him up and bodily threw him into the car, and said 'Keep your head down' ... there were girls clambering on the roof, and banging on the windows, and I was really afraid they would break the glass ... later, we heard that a girl had been injured in that scene – and another girl had been knocked down outside the Churchill. Alan saw that happen. She hit her head on a car bumper...."

By now, The Osmonds were big news. In two years, Donny and his brothers had sold 19,000,000 records. For this British trip, they had their first London concert set for the Rainbow Theatre on November 4th – with another one arranged for November 9th because tickets for the first show had sold out in less than twenty four hours. They also had other concerts scheduled at the Free Trade Hall in Manchester (6th) and at Birmingham Town Hall (7th). As well as these live appearances, they had radio and TV interviews, two bookings for the BBC

TV programme "Top Of The Pops" – though a personal appearance at the Swan and Edgar store in Piccadilly, London, had to be cancelled because the Police now realised that this would bring the city's traffic to a standstill.

During their fifteen-day stay, there were other problems – Donny and Jay were both taken ill with 'flu and then later it was discovered that Donny's voice was breaking.

It was part of Roger Holt's work to look after them during the trip, and he laid on tickets for Mr. and Mrs. Osmond and Marie to see the long-running London stage production of Agatha Christie's play "The Mousetrap" while Alan, Wayne, Merrill and Jay went to see Slade at the Rainbow.

"Only the managment of the theatre knew they were going," said Holt. "So they were able to mingle backstage and meet Slade, and they all got on together like a house on fire . . . they were really impressed by Slade, and I heard them talking together about instruments and music – just musicians' talk. . . . I heard Noddy Holder telling Alan how much he liked "Crazy Horses" . . . then another evening Alan went down to Tramps (a London discotheque which many leading actors and musicians frequent), and there he met Petula Clark, staying down there until 3 a.m. in the morning . . . another night Alan and I went to the Valbonne and the Speakeasy . . . then I took them all out for dinner at the Trattoria Terrazza in Soho – and even there the kids managed to discover that we were there having a meal, and a small crowd built up outside the restaurant . . . that was really funny because about fifteen fans stayed out there in the street until we'd finished our meal – and they all got their autographs."

Another day, Roger Holt arranged for London's most

exclusive department store, Harrods, to open specially for the Osmonds after normal closing time – because any normal shopping trips were by now out of the question.

"We just couldn't let them walk down a street any more – whatever the time, day or night," says Roger Holt. "I explained this to the Harrods security people, and they were very good about it . . . the Osmonds spent about £900 on clothes in the Way In department, which is Harrods' boutique."

Donny's bout of 'flu came on mid-way through another evening out when he went with his brothers to a special showing of the Burt Reynolds film "Deliverance". They stayed on to see the film while he was driven back to the hotel, and a doctor was called.

"It was discovered that both Donny and Jay had 'flu," Holt told me. "At one stage we thought we would have to cancel one of the concerts at the Rainbow. . . . Donny's temperature went up to 103 degrees . . . the doctor told us, 'If you want my honest opinion, he shouldn't do the show' . . . but Donny was very anxious that the show should go ahead, and he told his parents that."

So Holt set another security operation in train (this time without any of the fans or even the press rumbling it). He rented a suite at another hotel nearer the Rainbow so that the Osmonds could rehearse and then relax afterwards, especially Donny, without having to run the gauntlet through the Churchill's basement.

We had some anxious discussions over that show," says Holt, "because at the beginning, after Donny had come back from the cinema, we weren't really sure that it was 'flu. We were afraid that it might be something more serious . . . and after that other mix-up in Los Angeles when he was found to have acute appendicitis, we weren't taking any chances . . . at the crucial point we had a discussion together, their parents and me, and then went back into his room to see Donny. 'I'll make it,' he said, and, of course, he did – though we laid on an ambulance to get him away from the Churchill safely, and then that suite at the other hotel, and a doctor to make sure that he had as little strain as possible during the day."

One request that surprised even Roger Holt was when the brothers asked if he would arrange for them to see the pedestrian crossing that the Beatles had been photographed walking across for the album sleeve of "Abbey Road".

"I took them out to St. John's Wood in the car . . . we found the crossing in Abbey Road itself, and then they climbed out of the car and walked slowly across it in line, just as the Beatles had done for that sleeve photograph . . . and the pity of it was that none of us had a camera so we couldn't take a photograph," says Holt.

Another place where no fans ever traced them was in Bayswater – at the local Morman church, where they worshipped on the Sunday, just as they always do whatever part of the world the family happens to be visiting. And fans never knew that Donny was sitting up in the old press box watching Spurs on November 11th. But there was chaos again when the Osmonds went down to the London Weekend TV studios in Wembley to record four songs for a Christmas TV show. Hundreds of girls were waiting outside the entrance when they arrived, and then burst through the doors and ran wild through the corridors.

Meanwhile, Holt was sitting in the canteen with Alan and Donny, who had a can of near-beer shandy in his hand. Holt pointed to the words on the can, which said the shandy contained no more than two per cent alcohol.

"I've never had it before," said Donny.

When Holt pointed out the words, Donny turned to Alan and said: "That's alright, isn't it?"

But his elder brother, ever the dutiful Mormon, said: "I don't think you should drink it."

And Donny didn't.

Holt also travelled to Birmingham and Manchester with them, and noticed that the fans were even more noisy and violent outside their Manchester hotel than they had been outside the Churchill. "After the show in Manchester, there were so many kids outside the Free Trade Hall that I went up to the local Police Chief Superintendent and arranged for a Black Maria to be driven right up to the stage door, right over the pavement . . . and then we all climbed inside . . . but we could only move away very slowly because there were hundreds of girls pushing against the van . . . and the police were really nice, and the Osmonds signed quite a few autographs after that," says Holt.

On stage, the Osmonds had surprised the critics – playing their own instruments for some numbers with Donny seated at a Japanese organ, Jay playing Ludwig drums, Alan playing a Gibson guitar, Wayne on a Telecaster Fender and Merrill on a Fender bass. Then for other songs, they would put down their instruments, gather round the microphones and sing in close harmony – with a group of backing musicians they had brought over from America providing the accompaniment, leaving the Osmonds free to make the occasional dance movements as they sang.

At all four venues, the Osmonds were supported by a new British trio, Springfield Revival – and this proved the start of a very close working relationship. At the

Osmonds' own suggestion, Springfield Revival were signed to their own record label, Kolob; signed to tour with them throughout the United States and Europe in 1973; given the opportunity to record at the Osmonds' own studio in Los Angeles, and becoming through all this friends of the family (see chapter seven).

The shows themselves, the TV appearances and the enormous press coverage gave the Osmonds records – and particularly Donny's – another massive boost. When the family flew out of London Airport again on November 13th for concerts and TV shows in Bremen, Amsterdam and Paris, there was no doubt in anyone's mind. The Osmonds had been and conquered – and Polydor were soon to reveal that in 1972 alone, before their career in Britain had even swung into its full momentum, the Osmonds grossed well over £1,000,000 in record sales. They really were the biggest teenage pop phenomenon to hit Britain since the Beatles.

CHAPTER SIX

Before leaving London for those European concerts, the Osmond family agreed to the setting-up of a British-run fan club. This has since taken in all their fans throughout Europe – and now has a membership of nearly 70,000, making it the largest pop star fan club ever established in this country, even larger than those run on behalf of The Beatles and Cliff Richard in their respective heydays.

The person they recruited as its secretary was Mrs. Maureen Street, wife of a London music publisher, Ken Street, who used to be a musician himself, a member of the Original Checkmates. Now, he handles the songwriting catalogue of Guy Fletcher and Doug Flett, some of whose songs have been recorded by Elvis Presley.

Mr. and Mrs. Osmond were careful not to choose any of the commercial organisations that were keen to run a fan club for them on a profit-making basis. Instead, they took the view that the family was already making as much money as they needed – and the fan club should be run to provide a genuine service for Osmond fans. Choosing Maureen Street was to prove a wise decision because although Maureen had spent the last few years looking after her detached home in North London and bringing up her three children, she really did know all there was to know about running fan clubs – and far more than the Osmond family did themselves.

Back in the early sixties, she had worked as a receptionist at the Hyde Park Towers Hotel in Kensington, where out-of-town based groups often used to stay while visiting London. One of these was The Animals, who used to travel down together from Newcastle on Tyne in a delapidated old van to appear regularly at a club called The Scene in central London. Usually, they would spend the night at the hotel to give them the daylight hours next day to visit managers, agents, record producers, journalists, photographers, etc., before going on to their next gig.

They were already starting to receive occasional fan letters, and to help them out Maureen would often type out their replies for them late at night when work was slack, and she could sit down for an hour or so at the typewriter. Like so many of the groups of the time who had seen what The Beatles had managed to achieve, The Animals had endless confidence. Their singer Eric Burdon often used to say to her while Maureen was sitting at the typewriter answering fan mail: "When we're famous, you can be our fan club secretary."

Well, it happened. The Animals suddenly found themselves with a Number One hit "House of the Rising Sun". Within the space of two or three weeks, the group were STARS. The record was a hit throughout the world, one of the really big British singles of the mid-sixties – and Maureen, at their request, gave up her job as a hotel receptionist to work in their management office. She started running their fan club – and later organised others for The Dave Clark Five, Jimi Hendrix and Tony Blackburn.

And the one thing she impressed upon Mr. and Mrs. Osmond was that their club should be organised in such a way that members really felt that joining it had brought them closer to the Osmonds and, in effect, made them all feel part of the family. Before taking on the job, Maureen was invited to the Churchill Hotel to meet the family, and then Mr. and Mrs. Osmond went out to her home in North London – and were astonished when she said she could run the club from home using a desk in her living room, and an assortment of files and index systems in the garage. "We've got a computer to do all this back in Utah," said Mr. Osmond.

Even at that stage, before setting up the club, there were 17,000 letters to the Osmonds waiting in sacks at Polydor's offices – requests for autographs and signed photos, letters asking to join a fan club (even though none had been formed). Maureen read through them all, indexed all the names and addresses – and in January 1973, she had a mass-mailing, asking every single person who had written whether they would like to join the official Osmonds Fan Club. By mid-March, her paid-up membership had reached 23,000. By June, it was 45,000 – and by Christmas, 1973, the total had risen to 68,000. "I don't think there ever has been a fan club that has grown this fast," she says.

"I think the thing that surprised Mrs. Osmond most was that I said that they must have a regular newsletter," says Maureen. "This was something the American fan club had never had – indeed, it was something quite novel for American fan clubs . . . the traditional American fan club, so I'm told, made a charge for an initial membership, sent out a kit – and then became primarily a merchandising operation . . . but I stressed to Mrs. Osmond that to really succeed we would have to offer fans much more than that."

This is precisely what she has done – so successfully that the American fan club (which has 60,000 members, their names all fed into a computer at the Osmonds' offices in Provo, Utah), is also now planning to issue newsletters.

Running the British fan club, Maureen has employed four out-workers helping her to open mail and send off any goods that are ordered. The Fan Club handles a wide range of Osmond-endorsed products – red, white or yellow T-shirts in four sizes from £1.25 to £1.35; red or yellow canvas tote bags with Donny smiling across a zipped pocket for £1.50; white pillow cases with Donny's portrait and a message wishing "Sweet Dreams" for £1.10; satin scarves printed in red and black for £1.00; multi-coloured velvet caps, similar to those Donny has often been photographed wearing, for £1.20; a 71-page song book with the words and music to the "Crazy Horses" album, illustrated with photos of the Osmonds at home in Utah for £1.00; another song book with colour photos of Donny and the words and music of all his earlier songs for £1.00; original 10 in. by 8 in. photos of the group and individual members of the family for 25p each; writing pads with an Osmond motif on every page and stickers to go on envelopes for 25p; rings with Donny's portrait for 45p; charm bracelets, again with either a photo of Donny or Jimmy for 50p; medallions with a photo of Donny or Jimmy suspended from a 26 in. chain for 65p, and key rings with an Osmond photo on one side and the fan club emblem on the other for 25p. And in addition to all that, fans who belong to the club are able to buy all the Osmonds' albums and cassettes at ten per cent below the usual price.

All these are extras that members can buy if they want to. For the basic seventy five pence subscription, a first year member receives a brief biography of the Osmonds (which gives capsuled details of each member of the family), a colour poster, the newsletter (plus three vouchers to enable them to receive the year's other issues if they enclose a stamped and addressed envelope), a copy of the

Osmonds' secret code (through which Maureen sends coded messages to fan club members), a pin-on badge, a membership card and a black and white photograph with an inscription from the Osmonds welcoming them to the club.

Then in the second year, when renewing their subscriptions, members receive a large colour poster, a plastic wallet in which to keep their membership cards and secret code card, colour photos of Donny, Marie, Jimmy and their brothers to also go in the wallet, a certificate of membership with the facsimile signatures of each Osmond, an up-dated biography (with a glossy cover, twelve pages of facts about the family and a photo insert), vouchers for that year's newsletters, a letter welcoming their renewal of membership, and a plastic carrier with the Fan Club motif in which they can keep all their Osmond ephemera.

This is far more than any other fan club supplies to its members – but even this is only the tip of Maureen Street's fan club iceberg. Her flow of mail is never-ending – always at least eight sacks of letters a week. Each time, the Osmond family have been in London she has had to hire a van just to deliver their personal letters to their hotel.

Throughout the year, once a week, she air-freights gifts, letters and greeting cards to the States – she gets hundreds of letters from mothers asking for autographs for birthday cards. These are all included in the air-freighting and out in Utah, Mrs. Osmond sees that at least one member of the family signs the card. Then, there is another bulk-freighting back to this country so that Maureen can post the letters from London. "This saves a lot of money on postage," she says, warning that the whole process can take three months from the time she receives a request from a mother.

"Quite a lot of grandmothers write in asking me if they can get subscription forms for their grandchildren . . . and I'm always being asked for photos of Jimmy Osmond because older people think he's such a nice boy," she says.

The sort of questions she has to answer each week are mind-boggling, though apparently very important to the thousands of girls who want to know *everything* there is to know about their favourite Osmond. Are Donny's teeth real? Does Donny wear pyjamas in bed? Are any members of the family left handed? Who has the most fillings in his teeth? Can they walk down the street unrecognised? What time of day was each member of the family born? (an important question to members of the fan club, who diligently work out the astrological implications). Does Mrs. Osmond have a washing machine? How does Marie make lemon cake? Who looks after their horses when the Osmonds are away from the ranch? If Donny were to marry, what names would he choose for his children? What kinds of girls do they like? (A question that has to be answered many times a week). Does Jay like the Marx Brothers? Where do they buy their clothes? What colour is their hair? Which other singers do they admire?

Maureen also receives petitions from all parts of the country begging the Osmonds to make a concert appearance in that locality on their next tour. "I always send those on to Utah as well with my weekly sacks of mail so that these can be considered when the family are making their future plans," she says.

The newsletters themselves reveal other facets of what has become a very widespread organisation.

For instance, the December 1973 newsletter gave full details of the Osmonds' British tour, described their stage act, explained the security arrangements at London airport (and what had gone wrong), said which members of the Fan Club had been able to meet the Osmonds personally, revealed that they had signed over 12,000 autograph books for the fan club while they were here, gave details of forthcoming record releases (and summarised their past discs in the U.S.), answered thirteen questions on the wedding of Merrill Osmond and Mary Carlson, answered another twenty eight questions on various aspects of the Osmonds' life and career (their religion, what toothpaste and shampoos they use, their positions in the Mormon Church, their other relatives, a description of Donny's bedroom, facts about their herd of cattle, Marie's new fur coat – and had Wayne, Alan or Jay fallen in love yet, to which the answer was an emphatic "No").

Then there were names of members who wanted pen pals (including one in Indonesia), the recipe of Donny's favourite Chocolate Mint Ice Cream (which Mrs. Osmond had specially sent over to the Fan Club so that fans could try to make it, too, if they wished), details of two fan club competitions – one for a fan club song to be written to the music of "For He's A Jolly Good Fellow", and the other asking fans to work out which day of the week all the Osmonds were respectively born.

Then came gossip about the Osmonds, a suggestion that instead of sending Christmas cards to their favourite Osmond, fans might like to send them to the National Children's Deaf Society ("this doesn't mean they don't like getting your cards, as they do, but they do get an enormous quantity of cards and perhaps someone somewhere could truly benefit by just this small gesture.") Any fans wanting to know more about the Mormon Church are given an address to write to – and then each member was sent two unexpected gifts for Christmas, a plastic carrier bag with Donny's portrait on the side, and a free Christmas record with a specially recorded message from the Osmonds to their fans.

Certainly, there is no other fan club that tries so hard to keep its members so fully informed of every aspect and all the minutiae of artistes' lives and careers – but this is by no means the end of the story.

Maureen Street also helps to organise special projects suggested by fans, arranges for those who complete them to meet the Osmonds personally – and has a massive correspondence just answering questions.

"The letters are becoming much more adult now," she says. "At first, the letters were from very young fans, the weenyboppers as the papers called them. But now, I get letters from fans asking serious questions about their music, and there are now quite a lot of boys writing to me, possibly because of Marie, who is very popular. A lot of the newer fans are now over the age of eighteen. One of them, Angela, asked if she could help me at home so that I could cope with the daily correspondence better, and she comes in to help me daily now."

Occasionally, Maureen Street has minor "political" problems to deal with – such as the rumour that swept the nation's playgrounds that Donny had been killed in a car crash. "That's the sort of thing that nasty little boys spread around just to try and make their younger sisters burst into tears," says Maureen, who had many anxious letters which she quickly replied to, firmly quelling the girls' fears.

"And then we have all the different projects going on. These take up a lot of time."

For instance, two girls at Romford in Essex are collecting knitted messages from fans who each embroider their names on pieces of material four inches square, and then these are all being joined together by the two Romford girls to make one enormous scarf; another girl in Enfield is collecting sea shells, poems and jokes to assemble a special presentation volume for Jay; a girl in Walthamstow is organising a petition to the BBC asking that more Osmond records be played on the radio; a girl in Birmingham is making a presentation album of portraits of individual members of the Osmond family, each of them drawn or painted by members of the fan club; for Merrill's 21st birthday, a girl from Harrow was preparing a vast card in the shape of a key, decorated with the signatures of fans; a girl from Nottingham was making a picture postcard album so that fans all over Britain could each send in a postcard showing the area they lived; a girl in Thetford, Norfolk, is compiling an album of Disney characters; one in Birmingham is collecting individual letters from fans so that the Osmonds can be presented with one vast volume that will tell them who their British fans are, where they live, and what makes them so pleased to be Osmond fans, and a blind girl in Waltham Forest is translating all the Fan Club newsletters into Braille for the benefit of any other Osmond fans who may also be blind.

"I am very, very careful whenever a fan comes forward with a project like this," says Maureen Street. "The first thing I do is write to their parents to make sure that they know all about it and are prepared to give the project their written approval ... I think we must do this because some young girls might be swamped by the sort of response they would get, and would be unable to cope, which would be sad for her and would also make the other fans feel they had been let down.

"These girls sometimes just don't realise the scale on

which letters might start arriving. The very least I get is 8,000 letters a week. One girl down in Hampshire started making a felt snake from individual pieces of felt four inches square, and already the snake is over 100 ft. long and fills up most of her family's living room . . . so now her mother has suggested she starts making cushions instead!

"Then two other girls from Croydon started collecting signatures from fans planning to compile one large birthday card for Donny . . . well, the mail just came and came and came . . . so they had to make a huge card with folding pages attached, and they ended up with over 8,000 signatures. I took them both along to the hotel while the Osmonds were in London, and the whole family was absolutely amazed. When Donny saw that birthday card with 8,000 different signatures, he couldn't believe it – and he was very thrilled, too.

"All the girls were very nervous before meeting the Osmonds for the first time. I arranged to meet them all in advance, and then took them to the hotel and up to their suite . . . when they went into the suite, the girls were all tongue-tied for the first three minutes or so and wouldn't say a word. But the boys were all very good, very kind. They soon put them at their ease, and spent nearly an hour and a half talking to them all . . . and then we also presented each of the Osmonds with gold plated statuettes which I had bought on behalf of the club members . . . they cost £40 each, but there was enough money for that left over in the accounts at the end of the year."

Throughout the year, there are occasions – such as birthdays, wedding days and anniversaries – when Maureen Street gets a sudden deluge of mail. After Merrill Osmond had married schoolteacher Mary

Carlson in Utah, she received eight sacks full of presents for the couple. These she saved until the family arrived in London. Then Maureen hired a van and took all the gifts to the hotel. Merrill and Mary unpacked them all, and then went round to Harrods, bought four steel trunks, and had them all shipped back to their new home in Utah.

"It was quite amazing," says Maureen. "These fans wrote such lovely letters. They sent small gifts that they thought Merrill and Mary would like for their home – tea towels, toast racks, small cutlery sets, pillow slips, tray cloths, and dozens of ash trays, though neither of them smoke.

"I am always very careful never to accept any expensive gift without parents' permission. One young girl even sent me her mother's gold wedding ring, saying that Donny might like to save it for when he got married. I don't know how she got the ring – perhaps her mother left it on the kitchen table when she was washing up, I don't know. Anyway, I sent the ring straight back to her mother.

"I think you have to be very careful running a club like this because some of the girls are very young, indeed, and do not realise the consequences of some of the things they do. I am always getting girls sending in their childhood baby photos so that Donny can see what they looked like as children, but I always send them back to their parents because I realise they probably don't know the photos have been sent, and that it would break many parents' hearts to lose childhood photos like that.

"One girl in Scotland started knitting Arran sweaters for every member of the group – including Jimmy and Marie. That worried me a little so I wrote to her mother, who said this was quite all right. She knew all about it, and was quite happy because it kept her daughter off the streets! I get thousands of bracelets and love beads – and quite a lot of expensive Parker pens. Donny collects key rings, so a girl in Scotland is now collecting them all and compiling them on one large board to present to him next time he comes over."

The strange thing that Maureen has noticed is that many of the requests to start special projects, and much of the Osmonds' fanmail, comes from the North of England – particularly the industrial areas of Lancashire and Yorkshire, and from Liverpool and Manchester. "I should say at least seventy five per cent of the Fan Club's membership is concentrated in the North," she says.

The American fan club is run by the Osmonds' two elder brothers, Virl and Tommy. "Everything over there is organised within the family," says Mrs. Street, who comes in close touch with Virl and Tommy and especially with Mrs. Osmond who is on the phone regularly with information about different members of her family, supplying snippets for the newsletters, and keeping a careful eye on the quality of the various products issued to members, both in Europe and in the United States.

"These Osmond goodies are always cheaper than the fans would pay in the shops – and Mrs. Osmond insists on high quality. She has always been very anxious that people shouldn't cash in on the Osmonds and exploit the fans. Even in this country we've had one phoney fan club, and there was another occasion when forged tickets were printed for a fake concert in Glasgow. This is something that I am able to prevent as far as possible by organising the club in such a way that fans can always get genuine information about the Osmonds' shows and projects direct from me," says Maureen.

But there is still always the unexpected letter that may arrive in the morning mail – such as the one that arrived from two girls in Perry Barr, Birmingham, Susan Allsopp and Anne Marie Evans, who wrote:

> "We have been thinking of an idea for the Fan Club. As you know if the Osmonds do want to come back to this country, it may not be possible for them to land their plane at any airport because of the damage sometimes caused by us fans . . ."

So Susan and Anne Marie came up with an idea of their own – that the fan club should all band together, buy a site, and then build the Osmonds their own airport in time for their next British tour! And they added that this shouldn't require too much organisation as all fan club members would happily mark "Airport Donations" on the outside of the envelopes!

"You see that shows how careful we must be," said Mrs. Street. "The idea is obviously impractical, but those two girls believe it's quite possible for someone to buy the land to build an airport, and then actually build it in less than a year . . . they don't comprehend the actual money involved . . . how much land costs, all the planning laws, and the building regulations and the building costs . . . they don't think that's any difficulty at all. To them, the Osmonds need their own airport – so let's build it!

"Girls like that could be very easily conned if someone was unscrupulous enough to ask them to send money . . . you see, many girls are really in love with the Osmonds. They would do anything for them, and would go to quite extraordinary lengths just to contact them, to see them arrive at an airport ... one girl flew from Sweden just to see their concert at the Rainbow. Several flew over from Ireland to see them at Manchester, and a lot travelled from France ... and they are mostly very nice, ordinary, friendly girls, who just happen to love the Osmonds.

"When Merrill married, I had only about twenty nasty letters from girls threatening suicide and things like that – and then a few days later they all wrote to say how they had been thinking a lot about Merrill since they first wrote to me, and had now come round to the view that his happiness was what really mattered to them, and that if he really was happy then they were happy for him."

In all this, Maureen has clearly managed to make fans feel that by joining the Osmonds Fan Club they really do become closer to the Osmonds as a family. It has undoubtedly contributed to their success – and particularly to the sales of their records, and the circulation of their magazine "Osmonds World". The fact that she is so careful to avoid anything that might make parents feel their children were being taken for a ride helps to underline this.

"The Osmonds themselves couldn't be more helpful," she says. "When we made that Christmas record, I wrote a script for them and wired it by Western Telegram to Utah which cost me £60 ... for some reason, they never received it so I phoned the message over to Mrs. Osmond instead. Three days later the tape which they had made specially with that message arrived, and we were able to make the record.

"When they were in London, I took those 12,000 autograph books round to their hotel – and the whole group cancelled all their plans for the day, sat round a table together and started writing autographs. Every girl who sent in a book got at least one Osmond autograph – and Alan was especially good. He sat there for hours, writing even more than his brothers. I'm sure it's the fact that they genuinely care about their fans, and take so much time attending to things like signing autograph books and replying to letters and so on that gets through to their audiences . . . the girls really feel that the Osmonds *care*, and I really believe they do."

CHAPTER SEVEN

Those first British concerts by the Osmonds in November, 1972, proved the turning point in the career of another group, too – the British trio, Springfield Revival, who were booked to appear at all their concerts in London, Manchester and Birmingham. Thus began a close friendship that turned into a working relationship, too – with the two groups' tours and recording schedules being intertwined throughout 1973.

The trio had been formed in the summer of 1972 at the suggestion of Mike Hurst, a member of the original Springfields, who had been major recording artists in the early Sixties until Dusty Springfield decided to pursue a solo career. Hurst approached David Joseph and Keith Potger, who had already very successfully established the New Seekers. Joseph, an Australian TV producer and entrepreneur who had established his own management company in London, said later: "Mike had been toying with the idea virtually since the old group broke up, and felt that with a combined effort of our experience and his creative direction the project could be a highly successful one. We enthusiastically agreed with him and Springfield Revival were born before we actually found the members."

Joseph was already representing an Australian group the Mixtures, who had come to Britain on the strength of their hit "The Pushbike Song" – and from that group Melbourne-born Mick Flinn joined Springfield Revival. One night Joseph went down to the Theatre Royal,

Stratford East, to see Lionel Bart's musical "The Londoners" – and there he spotted Ray Martin, who had appeared in a TV series "The Incredible Adventures of Professor Brainstorm", had spent a year with the Royal Shakespeare Company at Stratford On Avon, and had first been discovered in childhood by Tommy Steele's father. He became the other male member of the trio. Then for their girl singer, Joseph and Potger recruited Donna Jones, a Manchester girl who had grown up with Lyn Paul of the New Seekers in a local singing and dancing trio, the Chrys Do Lyns.

In July, 1972, the trio made their cabaret debut and released their first single, "You'll Always Be On My Mind" (Polydor). In the August, they brought out their first album and started appearing on TV shows like "The Golden Shot" and "The Morecambe and Wise Show".

While their career was just beginning to take shape, David Joseph flew off to Los Angeles with the New Seekers, who were anxious to work in the States – and it was there that he met the Osmonds' manager, Ed Leffler, who told him the group were now planning their first live appearances in Britain, but had no idea which British artists they should ask to be the supporting act.

"I've got a group that would be just right," said David Joseph. "They're just starting ... they're a trio, and they're completely different to the Osmonds."

When he returned to his London office, Joseph promptly sent Leffler a copy of the Springfield Revival album plus their single and photos of the group. From that chance conversation a remarkable friendship has grown – Springfield Revival were contracted to appear on all the Osmonds' concerts in Europe, then they toured the United States with them twice during 1973, signed to their Kolob label, started recording at the Osmonds' own studio in Los Angeles, and were then invited to tour with them again when the Osmonds returned to Britain in October, 1973.

The two groups first met at the Churchill Hotel before the Osmonds made their concert debut at the Rainbow. That night, the Osmonds all stood at the side of the stage while Springfield Revival were performing. Afterwards, Donny told them: "You are going to be very big one day."

During that 1972 visit, the trio quite frequently visited the Osmonds at their hotel, travelled up to Birmingham and Manchester with them in their coach, and came to know them all closely. One night, the Osmonds took them all out to dinner – where Mick Flinn twice put his foot in it, twice forgetting that the Mormon religion forbad any kind of stimulant. First, he offered wine round the table – and then later, cigarettes.

"There was silence at first – and then they all burst out laughing," he told me, explaining that the Osmonds are in no way stuffy in their views, expecting other people to drink or to smoke in their company without feeling embarrassed if they do not join them. "While we drank wine, they drank milk," said Mick. "That seemed rather funny to me at the time – but Alan explained how strict the Mormon church was about things like that, and he said it in such a way that I didn't feel awkward."

The next March, Springfield Revival flew to Los Angeles to sing "Follow Me, Follow Me" at the American Academy Awards presentation ceremony on March 27th. The number was from the film "Little Ark", and had been nominated for the song writing Oscar. The trio shared a dressing room with Michael Jackson, and felt a little nervous playing to an audience that included many of their own childhood idols – film stars like Frank Sinatra, John Wayne, Charlton Heston, Rock Hudson, Shelley Winters, Diahann Carroll and Liza Minnelli. Already their manager was negotiating for the trio to tour with the Osmonds, and after the Oscars show, which was seen by 250,000,000 television-viewers around the world, they received this telegram: "THOUGHT YOU WERE FANTASTIC ON THE ACADEMY AWARDS SHOW STOP SEE YOU IN THE SUMMER LOTS OF LOVE THE OSMONDS."

Later, the Osmonds invited them up to their home in Westwood, Los Angeles, and as Springfield Revival stepped out of their car, Donny ran over and said: "Hi, it's great to see you again." Later, he and his brothers took Mick, Ray and Donna out for a meal at the Great American Food and Beverage Restaurant on Sunset Strip – and after they had eaten, the Springfields took their instruments out of their hired car, the Osmonds borrowed some in the restaurant, and they all started jamming together. "Donny had learnt the lyrics to several of our songs, which I thought was very flattering," said Ray. "We had a great evening together ... afterwards, Mick and Donna were invited back to the Osmonds' home to meet their parents again, while Donny took me down to see their new recording studio in Los Angeles, which had been built very much under his supervision – closely modelled on MGM's own studios, though this was much more luxurious than any other studios I've seen. There was a stage with separate soundproofing for Jay to record his drum tracks, and although the outside of the building was very normal-looking, once you stepped inside there were fitted carpets everywhere, and the very latest 16-track equipment, which had been installed to Donny's own specifications as the brothers accept him as the electronics wizard in the group."

Later, Springfield Revival started recording in that studio themselves, having long chats with the Osmonds about all those English clothes they had bought at Harrods and in Carnaby Street, about the differences between American football and English Association Football (which Donny had seen for the first time at that Spurs match), about their trip to Paris together (where Jimmy had been too scared to eat snails or oysters), about their fans in London and the crowd scenes, and about the Roller Derbies on TV, with teenagers flying round race tracks on skates ("That's really violent stuff," said Donny.)

"One thing that surprised me," said Ray Martin, "was that Donny and I were able to drive around Los Angeles without too much bother. Fans would keep running up to the car windows for autographs when we stopped at traffic lights, but Donny just signed them, and away they went, quite happy ... and it was interesting to see how nice he was to everyone he met, so friendly and natural ... he told me it worried him to think that girls sometimes slept out all night in the open or in their cars just to see him ... apparently, some girls stay outside the Osmonds' house in cars virtually 24 hours a day, taking it in turns to go and get food."

Of the Osmonds' Los Angeles home, which is a block of seven apartments in the suburb of Westwood, Mick Flinn told me: "It was all very normal once you got inside ... the only surprising thing that was there seemed to be Osmonds everywhere ... while I was sitting talking to Alan in the lounge, other members of the group would pass through, making drinks in the kitchen or whisking up a milkshake ... Donny would settle down and watch TV ... while Marie was ironing clothes, and her mother was looking after the cooking ... it made me realise what a big family they are."

Meanwhile, David Joseph and Ed Leffler had agreed terms for Springfield Revival to appear throughout the Osmonds' summer tour of twenty three American cities – and then later, they joined their autumn tour, too, before accompanying the Osmonds on their trip to Britain, France, Germany, Denmark, Sweden, Holland and Belgium. Then they later returned to America for a further series of concerts.

"The whole family are very nice to us," said Ray. "And we've had some incredible experiences together ... at Madison Square Gardens, there were 21,000 people packed into the stadium – and our manager David Joseph was nearly killed when one of the speaker cabinets fell over, and missed him by inches just as we were playing "Wig Wam Bam" ... he pulled the plug out of the mains because we had a 10,000-watt PA system that night, and that fused the mains ... we were just getting off stage when the mikes flashed, blinding us – it was belching smoke, an unbelievable sight ... and then we watched the Osmonds go on, and Donny insisted that the flash cables were attended to before they started playing ... they were all pretty frightened, because if something goes wrong with all that electricity around, someone could be killed ... some nights when we were touring, the Osmonds would invite us up to their floor for dinner – and one evening Donny invited us up to his room to watch the "Miss Teenage America" contest on TV ... and we've got a standing invitation to stay with them on their ranch in Utah."

Having spent so much time with the Osmonds, both

groups started to relax in each other's company – which gave Ray the chance to see a side to the family which few other people ever do. He found them warm and affectionate, always playing jokes on each other.

In Cleveland, Ohio, Donny surprised them all by dressing up as an old man with an old overcoat, hat, gloves and scarf – and then he walked out into the auditorium, sat down about four rows back in the stalls, and watched the audience filing to their seats. "We were all standing in the wings, watching him through the curtains – killing ourselves with laughter because there he sat, just before we were due to go on stage, with all these girls taking up seats around him, not knowing that Donny was just beside them ... he'll quite often dress up in funny clothes for a prank. When we played in Allentown, Donny thought his piano needed mending and so did the PA system, so he pulled on a coat and an old hat, wandered on stage with a screwdriver, and started mending the equipment ... everyone in the audience must have thought it was just a roadie, because no-one shouted out, or anything. And then Jimmy is also a great one for practical jokes ... he carries round a pair of protruding false teeth in his pocket, and when no-one is looking he'll slip them into his mouth, often giving people quite a start – particularly if they've never met the Osmonds before, and don't really know what to expect. When he's got those false teeth in, he looks like Larry Grayson.

"When we were staying at the Sheraton Hotel in Allentown, Pennsylvania, Jimmy got up to all sorts of tricks because he'd just been down to a joke shop ... he left a special soap on our wash basins that started to smoke when you washed your hands, and then he had some other soap that made your face go black ... then

onny waiting to change planes at Heathrow, October 1973.

Marie.

Above The Osmonds fly in and out from Holland, October 1973.

Below Donny at the Rainbow, 1973.

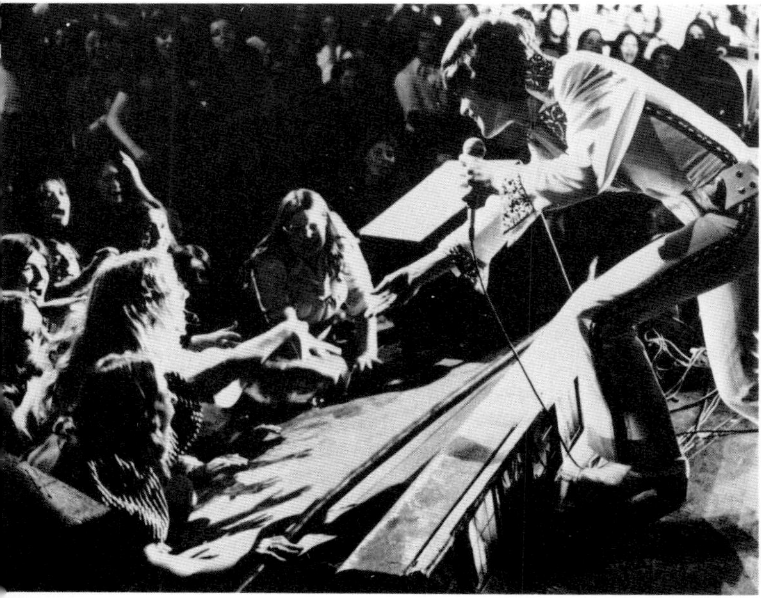

Jay.

e Donny at the Rainbow.

Below Jimmy at the airport.

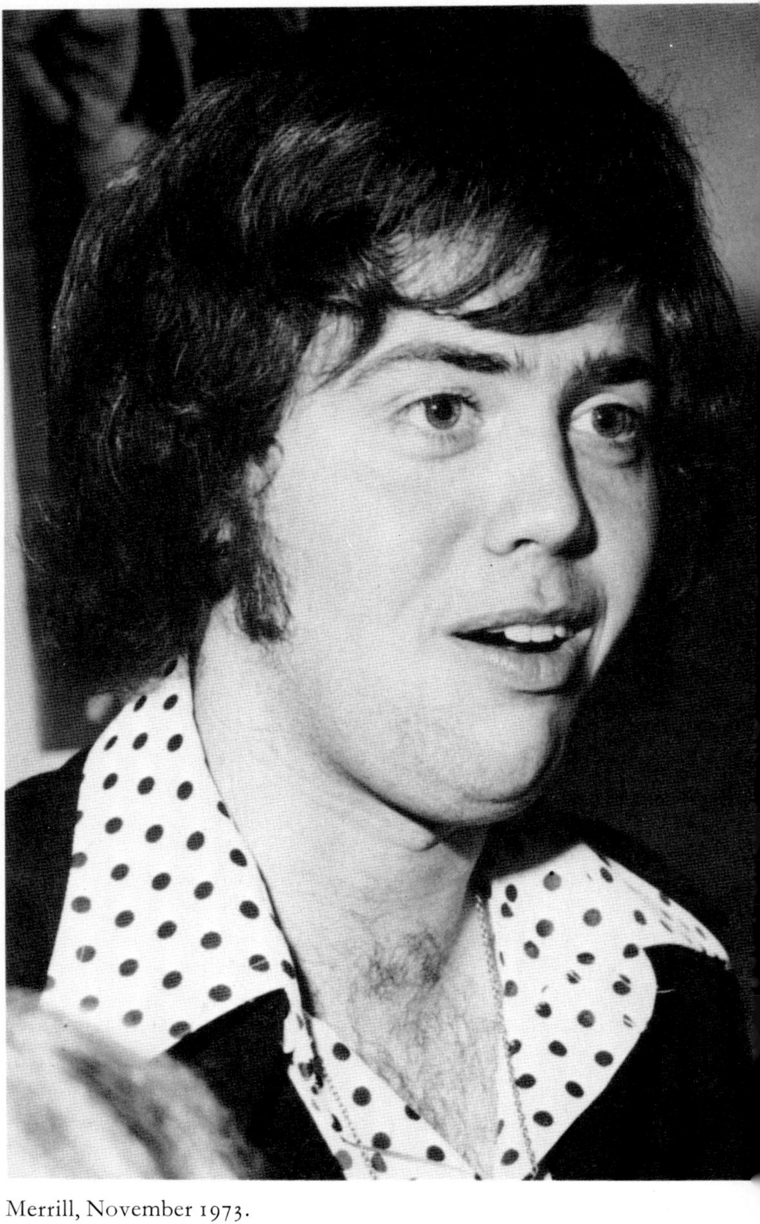

Merrill, November 1973.

Above
The Osmonds in concert, the Belle Vue, Manchester, 1973.

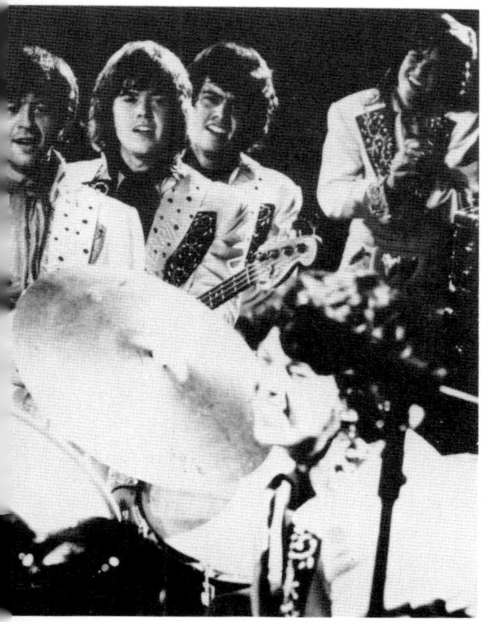

Below In concert again.

The Osmond family at Heathrow.

Family group. *From left to right,* Jay, Marie, Jimmy, Donny, Merrill, Alan.

Donny.

bove Donny and Marie.
low Donny signs his autograph.

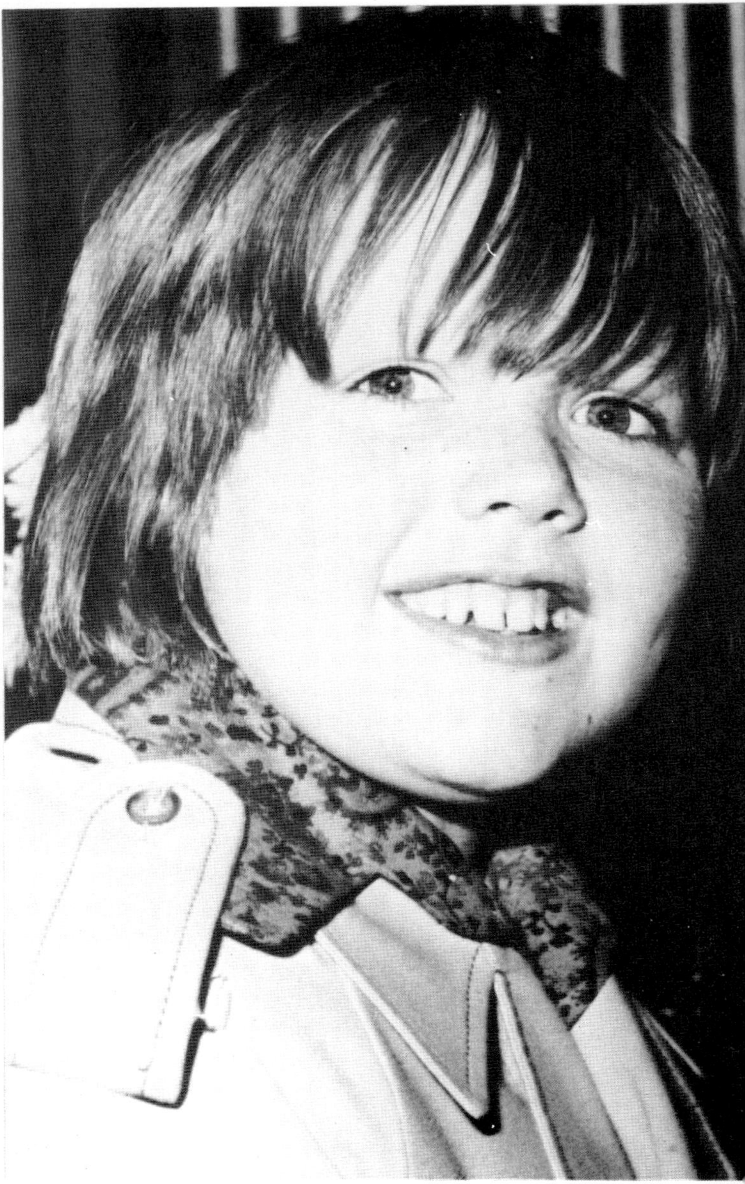

Jimmy.

Above Mrs. Osmond, November 1973.

Below Jimmy in concert at the Rainbow.

Above Donny.

Below Jimmy.

Ian, November 1973.

Above The Osmonds in concert.

Below Jimmy in concert.

he had an artificial ice cube with a dead fly in it, which he dropped in a bowl of ice . . . and then when he saw me, he sprayed me with a can of paint – and the paint just turned to foam after a while, and you could brush it off . . . he's a great bundle of fun, Jimmy – and he's learning karate and judo which gave me another surprise.

"When we were staying in Indianapolis, he threw me over his shoulder . . . often after gigs we would have a game of football while Marie and her mother went down to the box office to count all the tickets that had been sold to check that the Osmonds were getting their right percentage of the gate money . . . Donny tried to teach me his karate trick with wooden boards, but that went horribly wrong because I tried it in rehearsal and nearly broke my hand. But he did teach me a trick with a coin where you ask someone to hold out their hand, with a coin in the palm – and then ask them to close their fingers before you grab it. The secret is that you hit the hand in such a way that the coin bounces in the air – and that's when you grab it.

"All the Osmonds can do karate now, and it forms part of their stage act, with Donny and his brothers striking at wooden bricks . . . but they also do it as a hobby, because they find it relaxing, and because they've decided it's useful to have a form of self-defence in case they're ever involved in a difficult situation where they have to defend themselves, which is quite common in the music business where strangers will often take a swing at you because you've got long hair, or you're a musician, or because they don't like the fact that their girlfriends like you."

The Osmonds also showed Ray their collection of motorbikes at their home in Los Angeles – apart from

Jimmy, they all ride motorbikes. And Ray was astonished to see ten cars parked outside their apartment block – Alan told him that he had a Mercedes and that Merrill was planning to buy a Rolls, though Donny was as yet too young to drive on a public highway. "There's always cars standing by in case they need to go into town," says Ray.

Ray also met Merrill's wife, former school teacher Mary Carlson, who now tutors Jimmy and Marie when the Osmonds are touring, making sure they complete three hours' work a day on their different correspondence courses. "She's very extrovert," says Ray. "She's fantastic, always joking around, singing and dancing."

At Boston, while the Osmonds were on stage playing, Ray and Mary danced to the music from "The Plan" in the wings. "The girls are lovely in Utah, you know," she said. "I am going to have to marry one of them," said Ray. "Yes, you come to Utah and stay at our house," answered Mary, adding, "We'd love you to come and stay with us."

One thing that impressed itself on Ray was the way Alan Osmond was so clearly the leader of the group, taking decisions at concerts, arranging their PA system, and acting as their spokesman whenever they needed any special facility at hotels, airports or venues.

"Alan leads them in every way. I could see why because he is so together as a person. He falls naturally into it, acting as their spokesman – and answering the most questions when they are at a press conference. All the time, he leads – and I could see that particularly when they were rehearsing with Marie, who came on stage in France and America to sing her hit song "Paper Roses". He would show the others what was wanted, and they would do it . . . and in America when they are thinking of bringing a new number into the act, it is always Alan who phones Tommy Oliver, who does all their arrangements, and explains what they want done . . . of them all, I would say that Merrill is also a very good musician, really together on stage, and in rehearsals, showing his brothers what to do at some stages, whereas Wayne is much more easy-going, never worrying about anything."

Having spent so much time with the family, Ray and the other members of the trio each have a special souvenir to remind them of those tours together. After the American tour, each member of Springfield Revival was presented with a special gift, gold pens, each specially inscribed with the words, "THANKS FOR EVERYTHING. WE LOVE YOU – THE OSMONDS".

CHAPTER EIGHT

When the Osmonds returned to the United States after their European trip in November, 1972, they spent Christmas at home in Utah – with the main family excitement being the birth of Tommy's son, Benjamin Thomas, on December 16th. By then, Maureen Street was already planning the first issue of the Fan Club newsletter – and some days before the baby was born, Mrs. Osmond phoned her from Provo to say that the baby would be a boy. "She was absolutely sure of it – and very excited, too," says Maureen.

After Christmas, the Osmonds settled down to working on their next album, "The Plan" – breaking the schedule for just a few days when Donny and Alan flew to London with their father between February 28th and March 5th to appear on the BBC TV programme "Top Of The Pops", and to receive a special award from Polydor to mark the fact that they had sold over £1,000,000-worth of records in 1972, which was remarkable when one remembers that their records had only started to make an impression towards the end of the summer. While they were here, they bought more clothes, gave interviews to promote Donny's new single "The Twelfth of Never", paid flying visits to Amsterdam and Paris, and then returned to the States.

Even though their trip was unannounced – and the address of their hotel not published this time – news that the two Osmonds were in town broke in the national press, and another bout of Osmondmania erupted (making it very clear to Polydor that even more extensive security arrangements would have to be made next time the whole family visited London).

Fans seemed to know in advance as though by some form of telepathy where the two Osmonds would go next – something that has always puzzled those responsible for security. "Fans have the most extraordinary antennae. They're real detectives," says Maureen Street. "They soon work out which hotels the boys are staying in, when they will be going to a TV studio, which route they will take, when they will go to their record company offices, or go shopping . . . they seem to be able to work it all out with astonishing accuracy."

In the street outside Polydor's offices in Stratford Place, just off Oxford Street, vast crowds of girls waited in the street, shrieking, shouting, screaming and occasionally bursting into song with a lyric that seemed to have been composed spontaneously:

"We love you, Donny.
Oh yes, we do . . .
Donny, we love you."

At a press conference, Alan and Donny revealed that all the brothers were now being taught karate by American champion Chuck Norris (including Jimmy who was hoping to get his purple belt), that they would all be returning to Britain in the autumn, that they had liked what little they had been able to see of the English countryside on their previous trip. They also talked about the Osmond Foundation, which operates from Provo, Utah, and aims to help deaf children; their decision to appear in concert for President Nixon; their album "The Plan" (which Alan claimed would be "our Sergeant Pepper"), and their views on Alice Cooper, the American artist who sometimes conducts a mock-hanging on stage, performs strange acts with a snake, and even uses a guillotine as a prop ("I think he goes a bit too far," said Alan, somewhat predictably. "We'd rather come across with our music.") Of their religion, Alan said: "It's a modern church and we believe it has helped us a lot in our way of life."

Only one mistake was made at the press conference – in answer to one question, Alan said that because of death threats and warnings of possible kidnap attempts back home in the United States, the Osmond family were now seriously thinking of buying a house in Britain, and making their permanent home here. "We really like it in Britain," he said. "Everyone is much more relaxed and less aggressive. It would be terrific if we could buy a house and base ourselves in London."

That was good news for their British fans – but dismayed those in America, where the quote received wide publicity. And after their return to Los Angeles, Alan and Donny felt they had to call another press conference just to clarify what had been said. "It's true we have received those threats," said Alan. "And we do have a great deal of security wherever we go. But under no circumstances do we plan to move. America is our home . . . and we've called this conference to end the rumours, because everywhere we go our friends and our fans have been asking us about it."

The day before Alan and Donny were due to return to Los Angeles, hundreds of girls streamed out to Heathrow Airport, even running out on to the tarmac runways, hoping to see the two Osmonds. An airport security guard said: "About fifty of the girls rushed past the controls, swept past immigration officers and rushed past passengers." Five girls reached a plane bound for

Israel, and ran wild around the tarmac, alarming airport officials.

The next day when Alan and Donny flew to Amsterdam, there were even wilder scenes – which the two Osmonds tried to avoid by being driven right to the steps of their BEA Trident. An estimated 500 girls were running around the airport, and eventually police in squad cars and Land Rovers rounded them all up. "They shattered all our security precautions," said one official.

Back in the States, the Osmonds finished "The Plan"; discussed recording and future tours with Springfield Revival; appeared in cabaret at Lake Tahoe, Nevada; Donny recorded a solo album "Alone Together"; the group taped a Japanese TV commercial, and released the album; Donny recorded another solo single "Young Love"/"A Million To One" (released here on August 10); the group made that tour of twenty-three U.S. cities with Springfield Revival; Merrill met and married Mary Carlson on September 10, and on September 20, the Osmonds opened a three-week cabaret season at Caesar's Palace in Las Vegas.

By now, plans were far advanced for their next European tour – and in September Maureen Street sent out a special NEWS FLASH to all the members of the Fan Club, advising them that the Osmonds would be appearing in Manchester and Glasgow, with another London concert at the Rainbow. She told them that the Osmonds would fly to London from Scandinavia (after concerts in Gothenburg, Sweden, and Copenhagen, Denmark) on Sunday, October 21st and "because their arrival will be by private jet I do not have an exact arrival time, but it should be in the afternoon (which means any time after 12.00 noon). Their plane will easily be recognised because it has "Osmonds" painted all over it . . . if you'd like to welcome the Osmonds at the airport you should assemble at the Queens Terminal Building (younger members should be accompanied by their parents or older friends). Although I know it will be difficult to control your excitement you must all remember to be considerate to others using the airport and co-operative with Airport officials ... and (for the Rainbow concert for which the box office opened on September 22nd) tickets are priced £1, £1.50 and £2.50 and you can only get them by going to the Theatre box office in person. To avoid disappointment get there VERY EARLY!! Tickets are NOT AVAILABLE BY POST ... although there are only three concerts at the time of writing there is a chance that there may be more. Because I will not have time to write to you again I shall place an advertisement in the "Disc and Music Echo" music paper on either week ending 28th September or 5th October, so be sure to get both editions ..."

On the date given by Maureen Street for advance booking for the Rainbow concert, September 22nd, pandemonium erupted in the streets nearby. Girls had started queuing for tickets nearly two days in advance, and by midnight the evening before the tickets were due to go on sale over 10,000 fans were waiting in the street in pouring rain, blocking all adjoining roads, just hoping to get one of the 3,000 tickets for the show. At 11 p.m. that night, at the request of the Police, the box office was opened and all the tickets were sold – because by now it was quite obvious that any fans who arrived next morning at the advertised time would stand no chance of being allocated tickets with a queue 10,000-long already waiting. But such is the optimism of an Osmonds' fan that even after the last ticket had been sold, the waiting girls refused to go home – and by 5.30 a.m. in the morning fans were throwing any rubbish they could find at the theatre building, shouting, singing, threatening to burn the Rainbow to the ground, with the chanted chorus:

"We are going to build a bonfire
And put the Rainbow on the top,
Stick the manager on top of that,
And then burn the bloody lot . . ."

As breakfast-time approached, the crowd was starting to swell until there were again over 7,000 fans gathered in the street, refusing to believe that all the concert tickets had been sold. At 8.30 a.m. that morning, Maureen Street received a phone call at her home from the Police, asking her to come down to the theatre – but first she phoned Ed Leffler in Los Angeles, told him what had happened, and received his confirmation that providing the theatre was available the Osmonds would give another London concert for fan club members only. Then the Police arrived, drove her down to the Rainbow, where she was given a loud-speaker, and asked to climb up on the back of a Land Rover.

"It was absolutely unbelievable," she told me afterwards. "The crowd there was astonishing, and they were very angry because they couldn't get tickets, and because they thought the box office had been opened unfairly . . . I had told Ed Leffler on the phone that if the Osmonds didn't agree to appear at another London concert, someone might get killed down there . . . all the roads were blocked . . . buses and cars couldn't get through, and I was really worried. So I spoke into the microphone the Police had given me, and said it was

Maureen, the fan club secretary – and they all went quiet . . . then I said it was quite true that all the tickets had been sold the night before, and all the girls started to scream and shout . . . then I asked them to be quiet again, and explained that I had just phoned the Osmonds' manager in America, had told him what had happened, and that he had agreed to arrange another concert. I said that I would put all the details in the special advertisement in "Disc and Music Echo", and that if they listened to Radio Luxembourg, Tony Prince would give the details as well . . . and after I'd said that, the crowd started to disperse, and gradually all the fans went home . . . it really was terrible, though . . . if anything like that was to happen again, I don't think I could go on with this job. It was awful . . . I went back to the police station, and there was one girl there quite hysterical. She had been out in the cold and the rain for forty eight hours and had eaten no food, and I felt so sorry for her I gave her my husband's ticket for the concert . . ."

Worse was to happen when the Osmonds did arrive in October for that second series of live appearances. First, they flew to Scandinavia, for concerts at Gothenburg and in Copenhagen, again supported by Springfield Revival.

"There's one thing that stands out in my memory about Copenhagen – and that's a dinner we were all invited to," says Ray Martin. "I went along with Merrill and Mary, Donny, Jay, Marie and Little Jimmy. We had this raw smoked salmon brought to our table, and we just took one look . . . none of us wanted to eat it, but we didn't want to seem impolite . . . so Mary and Marie ate theirs, covered in this thick sauce, and we all struggled through ours, all pulling faces but trying hard not to show it . . . and the only person who did leave it was Jimmy."

The date of their arrival at Heathrow Airport had already been given to all the members of the fan club in that circularised NEWS FLASH, and several weeks in advance Maureen Street had been down to the Airport with Polydor public relations officer David Hughes to discuss the security arrangements. "They assured us that the fans would be quite safe, and just didn't share our anxieties," says Maureen Street. "One of the security officers told us, 'It'll be quite all right . . . we had 15,000 here when Frankie Laine arrived, and there was no trouble that day'."

But there was even though the cafeteria had been sealed off at the suggestion of the airport authorities, who thought the only danger would be in that area with so many plate glass windows.

On October 21st when the Osmonds flew into the airport, a crowd of girls standing on one balcony surged forward. Several coping stones fell from the balcony wall, and in the crush and the panic which developed among the 200-strong crowd of fans, sixteen were injured, with one girl having to have a kidney removed in hospital. Maureen Street was standing just by the balcony when this happened. "Hysteria broke out," she said, adding that when the first stones were dislodged the airport firemen arrived and removed all the other bits of coping stone that might also have been loose – and it was only after that that photographs were taken.

"The press took their photos after the stones had been removed, so it looked much more serious than it really was," Maureen Street told me. "There were about

10,000 girls there and Tony Prince and I had been playing music to them for five hours over the loudspeaker system ... we wanted to keep them calm and happy to avoid anything happening again like it had the previous April, when girls had been running wild on the runway ... it really was a fiasco, and the Osmonds were very upset when they heard that this one girl had been seriously injured, and would have to have an operation ... they sent her flowers and fruit at the hospital, and wanted to go down there to see her – but the doctors advised that this would cause the girl too much excitement which would be bad for her, so they said they would see her the next time they came over to London, and I'm sure they will – because they're all very good at anything to do with their fans."

This incident at the airport cast a shadow over that tour, with hostile questions from press and TV reporters, and a general feeling that Polydor and the Fan Club should not have advertised the Osmonds' arrival – but the concerts themselves were a great success, and the group did give an extra show at the Rainbow Theatre on October 30th for fan club members only to make up for the confusion that had broken out back in September. The morning after the second concert, the Osmond family flew out to Paris where they based themselves at the Georges Cinq Hotel throughout the remaining dates of their European tour.

While in London, Donny filmed TV appearances to promote his latest single, a revival of the old Nat King Cole number, "When I Fall In Love" coupled with "Are You Lonesome Tonight?" – and Marie was filmed singing "Paper Roses", which had already been a No. 1 hit for her in the States. As a group, the Osmonds also had their own hit "Let Me In" coupled with "One

Way Ticket to Anywhere", taken from their album "The Plan".

The Osmonds also met those fan club members who had completed special projects, compiling photo albums and birthday cards for Donny; signed those 12,000 autograph books, and Alan was again able to spend a couple of nights down at different clubs, where one evening he was photographed talking to blonde Scandinavian actress Lena Skoog, estranged wife of former Marmalade drummer Alan Whitehead (which provoked an angry mailbag for Maureen Street, who gets hurt, complaining letters every time a press report links any one of the Osmond's names with a girl, either romantically or otherwise). Throughout this trip, it was very difficult for any of the Osmonds to have much privacy – every day thousands of girls stood in Grosvenor Square, looking up at the windows of the Britannia Hotel where they knew the family were staying. Often they would surge across the street, stopping all traffic when what they thought was an Osmond appeared at a window. Shopping was quite out of the question. The Osmonds were virtual prisoners in their rooms – although they were able to move around more easily on the Continent, as Ray Martin of Springfield Revival recalls:

"We had flown to Sweden with very few extra clothes, and it was really cold when we got off the plane. Marie hadn't brought a coat with her, so Mr. Osmond went out and bought her a beautiful fur coat in Copenhagen, and Merrill and Donny bought new coats, too ... wherever we went in Europe, Marie collected china dolls – especially in Copenhagen where she also bought salt shakers, pepperpots and other ornaments in the local porcelain, as well as shoes. She really goes mad with money, whereas Donny is much more careful –

though even he bought loads of clothes in Paris.

"In Brussels, Marie bought some lace to take back home to Utah. She just freaks out with money when she's shopping. When I told her that Brussels was famous for its lace, she said, 'Oh, I must have some then' – and went straight out and bought loads of lace handkerchiefs and a scarf ... Donny bought himself the most fabulous dark brown leather coat with a mink fur collar and some trousers."

Something else that Ray noticed about the family was Little Jimmy's memory. On a previous trip, Jimmy had taken a fancy to the dungarees that Ray was wearing. "He just fell in love with them. He hadn't seen anything quite like that before, so I promised to get him some ... I saw him again three months later, and the very first thing he said to me was, 'What about that bib and braces?' He's got a fantastic memory – so I just had to go out and get some for him. I found them in Carnaby Street, and when I gave them to him his mother insisted on giving me the money for them."

So much happened to Springfield Revival during 1973 because of their association with the Osmonds, so many concerts, so many plane flights to new cities, so many nights spent at strange hotels that Ray's memories now are quite fragmented; he cannot place it all in sequence. Different cities bring back isolated recollections. Of this European trip, he remembers that they flew to Frankfurt for a concert "that was very weird. When Donny was singing 'Puppy Love', which usually has all the girls swooning, the audience just sat in their seats and looked at him ... but Donny knew just what to do. He left the stage, walked down into the audience, kissed some of the girls in the front row, and you could feel the audience warming towards him ... in Berlin, the audiences were much more hysterical – and in Hamburg even more so.

"In France, we played this awful place in Lille, very big, all glass – with paraffin heaters everywhere to keep it warm. The sound balance was really atrocious ... in Lyons, the audience was only about three-quarters full, but all our other shows in Lille and Paris were sold out ... we stayed at the Georges Cinq Hotel in Paris, which was beautiful, with deep piled carpets everywhere, and draped curtains, like a palace. It cost £50 a night for each of us, and the Osmonds all shared ... Donny and Jay were in one room, Alan and Wayne shared another, and Merrill and his wife were in another.

"Every night, we all had dinner together around candle-lit tables and we had a little competition to see who could blow out the most candles ... Donny could only blow out two first time, and then Alan could only blow out one, and then Donny had another go and blew out three ... that's something that will always stick in my mind whenever I see a table with lighted candles ... but the food there was so incredibly expensive ... one evening, just three of us went out for a meal, not a very exceptional meal, and it cost us £69 ... Marie bought herself a travelling case and a vanity case while she was in Paris, which made Merrill laugh because he said she was always spending money.

"Alan bought himself a Nagra tape recorder, which we tried out on the way to Le Bouget airport. John Rosenberg, one of their backing musicians, brought his trumpet out of its case, and we all sang "Happy Birthday To You" because it was Ed Leffler's birthday. That turned into a real sing-song with Wayne playing guitar, and Dennis Greig, another of their backing group, on clarinet ... later we had a great big chocolate cake like a mousse as a birthday cake, and for a joke Donny covered his face in chocolate so that he looked like one of the Black and White Minstrels ... when we were up in the plane, which was the same Caravelle that David Cassidy had hired to tour Europe, and even had its own visitors' book, the pilot asked us if we'd like to sit in the cockpit, and Wayne told me all about his flying lessons in Utah, and the plane that he's buying ..."

The European tour was certainly their most successful, with the Osmonds, Donny and Marie all entering the charts, but the family were far from happy with the security arrangements – and it seems certain that those scenes at London Airport will prove to have been the last of their kind, because the British Airports Authority were so shocked by the accident that they are now considering banning all organised welcomes for visiting pop stars. A spokesman for the BAA, after hearing that precise details of the Osmonds' arrival had been circulated to fan club members, said: "This was irresponsible and courting danger." And it now seems certain that on future tours, the Osmonds will follow David Cassidy's example – and have all their movements in and out of the country kept secret.

CHAPTER NINE

While the Osmonds were in London, they gave several press conferences – each to a different group of journalists, one day to the national papers, another to the trade press, and another to the teenage magazines. These were held in their suite at the Britannia Hotel, just around the corner from the American Embassy, with Grosvenor Square behind their windows. Throughout that week, thousands of girls stood in the square, screaming for the Osmonds to come to the windows – which they occasionally did. Each time, their fans would surge across the street stopping all traffic.

I attended one of these conferences, and it was an improbable occasion – with the Osmonds all seated on burnt gold settees around two walls, with gold Italianate mirrors, a Georgian-style print above them of a gentleman in dress uniform with a sword, a basket of dahlias and carnations at their elbow, brass lamp standards and beige shades providing the lighting – which was magnified by the arc lights needed by the film camera team covering their tour for a BBC TV documentary. These occasions are invariably banal, which is as much a joke to the journalists as it is to the artists – the first question was: "Have you had any hit records?" To which Donny replied: "Marie had the last one!"

Donny was sitting there, between his brothers – wearing brown denims with studs down the seams and a blue check shirt. Merrill wore a blue suit with a cream shirt. Jay, a red, blue and orange check shirt, and Alan and Wayne were in slacks and shirts. At first, Donny seemed a little awkward, fingering a mark on his cheek left by a fake "scar", which he had affixed as a prank. "I was trying to scare the security guards – and then afterwards I couldn't get the glue off. Now, I'm beginning to look like Frankenstein," said Donny. At first the questions came slowly, as they often do at press conferences. I kept a shorthand note, and here is an almost verbatim account:

About their karate and the stage accident

Alan: Jay is the karate expert of the group, though we've all got blue belts now.

Jay: I got my nose broken in Indianapolis, where we were playing to about 15,000 people. The show was going quite well, and we carried on after the accident.

Alan: I hit him. I fractured my knuckles – and he broke his nose in four places. I gave my brother a bloody nose. He went down, and we didn't know for sure that it was broken, but we had to finish the show.

Wayne: He got really plastered. Jay's blood was all over the place.

Jay: I bruised my ribs as well.

Alan: He was really bloody, but we finished the karate number. After the concert, Jay and I were driven to hospital in a police car. There, they sewed up Jay's nose and my hand.

About their fans

Donny: We wish we could see all our fans. They like to see us, and we would like to see them.

Alan: We didn't like what the papers said when we arrived here. They made that incident at the airport look more than it had been. There had been people out there inciting the kids for a picture. I think that's wrong. They were looking for headlines. The security problem now is really a challenge, and they make it very difficult for us.

Their Christmas plans

Alan: We try to spend Christmas at home now. We told our manager Ed Leffler that we wanted to spend Christmas at home last year and this year. We're hoping to spend every Christmas at home.

Their film plans

Alan: We're working on an idea for a film right now. We're working on the script. But we don't want to do a movie just to be in the movies. We've found an idea that we think artistically is a step forward for us. Maybe, we'll also do a documentary of The Osmonds Story, just to show where we are right now. But a major film would have to be a step forward.

Wayne: We would like to do a movie ... there is a person writing a script for us right now, and that's the first step.

Ed Leffler: I think we can say that the person who is writing it has already won an Academy Award.

Donny: I want to play James Bond. Jay wants to use karate – he gets a kick out of it!

Alan: The film wants to be a vehicle for several songs. That's the obvious thing.

Wayne: We could be actors.

About their ranch

Alan: Our father has brought over this breed of cows from Switzerland, Simmental. We've also got about forty horses, and we do a little horse back riding.

Donny on his electronics and his bedroom

Donny: I have always had this thing about electronics. My bed is on a motor and rises up to the ceiling, and then goes on to a shelf . . . then I can close doors around it. Underneath my bed is my laboratory. My bookshelf rises up and down, too, and I've also got an elevator that takes me up to bed . . .

Jay: He gets a lift out of it.

Donny: It takes me up on a platform. We've had so much done to our home now. I've got 24-track recording equipment installed in the basement, and we've spent a lot of money on it. That's to make sure we've got an excellent recording studio.

Alan: We like to be at home. Utah is our home. We only go to California to record.

Wayne: The kitchen has been designed just the way our mother wanted it. There's a great big round table in there so that the whole family can sit around at breakfast – and there's a garbage masher . . . we have a TV room up in the loft so that Jimmy can take his friends up there to watch TV without disturbing the rest of us.

On women's lib

Alan: A woman's place is in the home. I would like my wife to cook for me and raise my family. I believe a man is definitely the head of the family.

Merrill (The only married member of the group). I can vouch for that.

Merrill on his marriage to Mary Carlson

Merrill: I did not really propose to her. It was like

a thing we did talk about. We decided after our last tour in the States. The day I got back, I said to her, "Well, what do you think?" I had known Mary for about four and a half months before we got married. Before I met her, I'd made up my mind that I wouldn't get married for at least eight years – but then we met!

Donny: We tease him all the time – he's an old man now!

Merrill: I've been very surprised by the reaction of our fans. It's been very favourable, and we're delighted with that.

On who will be next

Donny: Probably Alan – he's the oldest.

Alan: It'll be Jimmy!

Jay: He's looking right now!

Merrill on his new home

Merrill: I've just bought a house in Provo about a mile and a half away from the rest of the family. It's really nice with three bedrooms, a den and a living room. I saw the house, and then phoned up the man who was selling it.

On their free time

Merrill: We took the whole of June off, and we didn't do much after the August tour until we came here ... we had one day off this trip, and I took Mary to the Tower of London to see the Crown Jewels ... then we went down the Kings Road.

Donny: I bought a couple of coats, and then stopped in the park and played a little bit of soccer.

Alan: The trouble is the Police want to know everything we do, all the time.

Donny: I like American football, but I'd like to play

soccer here, too . . . we call it soccer in the States now.

Jay: He wants to be a quarter back in a year's time.

On photography

Donny: We've got a dark room in our house. We can develop our own film after we've taken pictures.

On Wayne's interest in flying

Wayne: I'll be able to fly commercial planes soon. I'm getting a commercial pilot's licence.

Donny: He helped to fly our jet for the whole of the European tour.

Alan: The airport in Utah wants to hire him as an instructor.

Wayne: I've already got my own plane which I'm going to keep in Utah, and soon I'll be able to fly it myself. It's a 182 Skyline, a single engined plane.

Jay: He wears cotton wool in his ears when he's flying so he can't hear a word you say.

Wayne: That's just when I'm flying into airports.

On whether they appeal to older audiences

Alan: We would like to feel that we reach different audiences – and that includes older people. We already do that when we appear in cabaret, with a very different sort of show to the one we do in concert.

Donny: In France we are known as a heavy underground band – much more so than here. I think we would like to break out in other areas, but as we do so we would like our fans to move ahead with us.

Merrill: That was why we wrote the album "The Plan" ourselves, which created interest in us as songwriters. It showed what we could come out with.

Alan: That's something we have learnt on this tour; a lot of older people are now listening to the Osmonds.

Merrill: I think our demographic area has changed.

Donny: It's Alan, Wayne and Merrill who do the writing – and maybe Alan will start something else. There are lots of different things we could do.

Alan: Sometimes Merrill and I will write a song, and then Wayne will maybe do the lyrical line. We work it out together. It's something that goes on around the house – wherever there's a tape recorder, and one of us has an idea for a song. Things happen like that. Our whole life revolves around music . . . you see, we're working in four demographic areas. There are four acts within the Osmonds family – there's the Osmonds, Donny Osmond, Jimmy Osmond and Marie Osmond, and we each appeal to a different age range.

Merrill: I love classical music.

Jay: You can be knowledgeable about each phase of music. This can only enhance the music you are into.

Merrill: Everything goes into it, and yet nothing does. It's a "square" thing more than anything. Some influences can be restrictive. With our LP "The Plan", all we expected was the heavy things, but more came out of it than that because of all our different influences.

About the songs in their stage act

Alan: For this trip we worked out an act that would appeal to older people. That's what we did putting the show together. We now have a two-hour concert act, and that meant choosing from about eighty songs. That was a problem. Now we've decided to sing about half-an-hour of pop stuff, and then we do "The Plan".

About the timing of their concerts

Alan: That's something we had to think about, because if we finished too late any girls living outside London would have to hitch hike home. That means they get home too late – so that's why we have an early show.

On Attempts to book a larger venue

Merrill: We came up with too many problems trying to book an outside venue. There were ideas put up for it, but these fell through.

Alan: That's one of the problems of performing here. We tried to book the Wembley Pool, but that was unobtainable. There were some Russian gymnasts appearing there. Then there was an idea for a mammoth show at Earls Court. The trouble is finding somewhere that can bring in enough people . . . we wanted to perform in some other places (Bristol was one), but at least we know this TV show will reach millions. We'd really like to take a chance and appear somewhere new.

On their views on those Mormon Church leaders who had described pop music as depraved

Alan: We are not. We don't do anything that would be degrading.

On going to church

Donny: We try to go to church services whenever we can. Wherever we go, we always go to church. We went to church yesterday – to a Mormon temple outside London. No-one knew we were coming. We try to stay as active as we can.

Alan: We are active. We can do pop music and speak. This is the thing in the Mormon Church. There is no basis of a paid clergy. There is a basis of people within the Church. It's much easier for us if we are singing rather than talking.

Donny: Our two elder brothers have done two-year missions. Alan would have been the next to go on a mission.

Alan: I can create more love and brotherhood through our music. If a missionary goes out, he knows his own responsibilities for two years. I wanted to go very badly, but this is the best medium.

On why Donny records standards made famous by other artists

Donny: This next single, "When I Fall In Love", was an old Nat King Cole number, and I've recorded another album.

Alan: They are all new songs to Donny.

Donny: This is the second Nat King Cole number I've done. The first was "Too Young".

On their stage act

Alan: As I've said, we're really two different groups. There's Donny's audience which is specifically for what he's doing ... we're always trying new things. We try to stay one step ahead of our fans if possible. If we are good musicians, then the fans will grow up with us. In two years, we'll have an older audience – just as The Beatles took their audience right with them.

On Donny's voice breaking

Donny: That happened when I was recording "A

Time For Us". I've done over a dozen songs with my new voice ... I was worried that my voice was breaking.

Jay: His voice changed really gradually.

Donny: That happens to a lot of people.

Alan: It was a favourable, a suitable voice change ... when Jay's voice changed, he went from tenor to bass.

Donny: I felt my range creeping in a little. There was that number on my last LP, "A Time For Us", where I could feel it.

On Donny going out with girls for the first time

Donny: (Who was told he could start after his sixteenth birthday). I am going to go on a date – if you know anyone, ring me up!

On Christmas

Donny: That's the time of the year when the whole family get together with Aunt Mary. It's a great big family get-together. A very enjoyable time for us.

Merrill: We open our presents at 4 a.m. in the morning.

Wayne on his new plane

Wayne: Before I can use the aeroplane, I have to fly it 1,500 miles from Wichita, Kansas, to Utah.

CHAPTER TEN

Whever one meets the Osmonds all together, whether it be in a hotel lounge or a TV studio, it is very obvious that Alan is their leader, their spokesman, and is accepted as such, possessing confidence and a natural authority. At press conferences, it is Alan who fields the awkward questions about the family religion or fans being injured; in rehearsals, it is Alan who takes command when something goes wrong.

No-one seems to mind this within the family; his brothers call him "Big Al"!

Alan, who is now the tallest member of the family standing 6ft 1in and weighing 10st 10lbs with dark brown hair and brown eyes, was the third son to be born to George and Olive Osmond when the family were still living in Ogden, Utah, in that first home that Mr. Osmond had had built to his own specifications, while he worked away at his insurance business, his post office and his real estate.

When Alan Ralph Osmond was born on June 22nd, 1949, his eldest brother Tommy was already nearly four years old, and his other brother Virl was nearly two. The birth of this third son had been awaited with some anxiety because Tommy and Virl had both been born with defective hearing, and Mrs. Osmond was naturally anxious about her next child, hoping that this would not prove to be something that ran through the family, though she was already helping her two boys overcome their disability.

"We've always realised that we have quite exceptional parents," Alan Osmond once told me. "They have brought us up very well, taking great care with our education and our health.

"Because my two elder brothers were both born hard of hearing – Virl has a sixty per cent loss of hearing and Tommy has a twenty per cent loss – our mother taught us how to speak with sign language, and this was something that she taught to every member of the family . . . now it comes in useful other ways . . . when we're at either end of a crowded room, we can 'talk' to each other in sign language," said Alan, and I was later to see this in action, when Mr. Osmond suddenly started 'talking' across a room to Marie.

Although the handicap was a very real one for Tommy and Virl, Mrs. Osmond tried hard to overcome it. She taught them to produce sounds, using a vacuum cleaner to demonstrate the relationship between vibration and sound. Later, she taught Virl and Tommy to tap dance and to play the saxophone. But there was never any question of Virl and Tommy being able to be a permanent part of the Osmond Brothers group. "There's a permanent nerve loss, and that's why they can't hear properly," said Alan.

For the Osmond children, deafness was not the handicap it has been to many others; there was always so much happening at home with Mrs. Osmond's schoolrooms, her music lessons, her vegetable garden, her home cooking, Daisy the cow and fruit in the orchard.

"We always used to do an hour or two's work around the home before going to school, and then we'd work again in the evenings, and there'd be our homework to do, too," says Alan. "But we never ever felt that we had nothing to do. That was the important thing. There was always something happening."

Alan learned to paint and studied photography, took up guitar (he is the Osmonds' lead guitarist), and also learned pinao, banjo, saxophone and bass guitar. And the other unusual aspect of family life with the Osmonds was that his mother always insisted on a properly balanced daily diet of vitamins, to a rare degree of accuracy.

"Our mother has always been into health foods," Alan told me. "It was something she was very strong on throughout our childhood, making sure every day that we had our vitamins. This all starts with our beliefs, really, because the Mormon Church is very strict about the substances that you allow to enter your body. That's an important part of our religion.

"We believe that our bodies were never intended to have artificial stimulants . . . that's why we never drink alcohol. We never touch tobacco. Coffee and tea are also forbidden, and so is Coca Cola because that contains caffeine, which is a stimulant . . . the doctor once recommended tea to me, and I had some, but that was purely medicinal. At all other times, we are against it . . . I did drink some Coca Cola once, and I didn't dislike it, but that was an accident.

"When we were younger and still living at home in Ogden, our mother used to be able to look after our diet more easily because we grew our own fruit and vegetables, reared our own beef, had our cow Daisy, who provided us with the milk to make butter and cheese. But, of course, it's much more difficult with all the travelling we do, so now our mother makes sure we have our vitamins a different way.

"Every day, we each eat four almonds because they

contain a lot of vitamins – it's like a natural multiple-vitamin pill. And then we always have Vitamin E every day because that's so important . . . Wayne even takes Brewer's Yeast every day, but I don't go that far . . . and we drink a lot of milk or orange juice . . . our mother often carries a lot of these things around us because it's sometimes difficult to get them when you're travelling from one city to another, and unable to leave the hotel."

Alan is sure that this is one of the main reasons the family is so healthy. "I've only ever had to miss two shows," he told me. "And that was after a long plane journey, when I started to feel dizzy . . . but apart from that, I've never missed a show."

As the eldest member of the group, now in his twenty-fifth year, Alan is a constant source for speculation; will he be the next to marry. In the past year, his name has been linked with Eve Graham of the New Seekers and also with Karen Carpenter; he has been seen with different girls at the London clubs, and was photographed at one with Lena Skoog, estranged wife of former Marmalade drummer Alan Whitehead.

"But I don't think he'll marry a girl in the music business," says Maureen Street, who as European Fan Club secretary has to answer letters from miserable fans every time Alan is seen with or reported to have been with a girl.

"I expect the girl he marries will probably be a member of the Mormon Church – just as Merrill's wife was – because the whole family are very strict about their religion . . . Alan is now an elder of the church, and he was the only one of the brothers allowed to attend Merrill's wedding for that reason . . . but for the success of the group, he would have gone on a Mormon mission by now, so I think religion would probably play an important part in any decision he made about getting married."

Alan himself says that the qualities he looks for in a girl are "femininity, grace, a good sense of humour, someone who can share my interests, and is always herself . . . someone who is always quite natural. I like girls who believe in themselves and have strong opinions of their own, and when I do marry I'd like her to be the sort of person who would want to travel with me, and someone who understands that our career is such that it makes a lot of demands."

I then asked him whether the Mormon religion would prevent him marrying someone from another faith. His answer was not direct, but gave a clear indication that Maureen Street's analysis is probably correct. "To me my religion is a way of thinking and a way of believing," he said.

"It's a way of life. That's what it is to me, and that's something I would want to share with someone I married."

CHAPTER ELEVEN

Merrill is the most easy-going Osmond, instantly friendly with a memory for names and faces, a relaxed way of speaking, something of a weight problem (he's naturally chubby), and he is also the only married member of the group. Even before his wedding, he seemed anxious to escape the pressures of touring to lead a more settled life.

During long discussions with him when the Osmonds toured Europe in the autumn of 1972, it was very apparent that the thousands of fans laying siege to their hotel was an aggravation that he would happily have lived without, though he never expressed himself so bluntly; the Osmonds never do. Just as their own image seems to be too good to be true, so their fans are always said to be marvellous, wonderful people who are only demonstrating love, sincerity and enthusiasm.

But, as I say, Merrill seemed the first member of the family to be slightly disenchanted. "The security is unbelievable now," he said, a little glumly. "Wherever we go, we have to stay up in our hotel rooms . . . usually, the whole floor of the hotel is booked so that the security guards can seal off the elevators and the staircases, but it still means we can't go out.

"If we do try to go out, they'll rip our shirts . . . in Chicago, we even got pulled out of the gates of an elevator. We were just walking over, and a girl screamed and that was it . . . it means we can't even go shopping so if we want to buy some clothes then our mother goes shopping for us. She will be going to Take Six to see if she can find some clothes for us ... that's not such a problem in the States because there all our clothes are supplied to us by Male Pants, and we don't have to go shopping for them.

"There are other things that I have to miss. I would have loved to have seen the Tutenkhamun exhibition, because I've always had this interest in ancient Egypt, the Pharaohs and archaeology, but that's out of the question ... just imagine what would happen if we queued up in the street outside the exhibition! ... I'd like to be able to go to the British Museum, as well, and the Science Museum – because that's the sort of thing that interests me, but that's out, too ... we were able to see a few museums when we visited Germany," said Merrill, who shares the Osmond enthusiasm for self-improvement.

He was born on April 30th, 1953, when the family still lived in Ogden, Utah. Now, he is 5ft 10in tall, has light brown hair, hazel blue eyes, plays bass guitar when the group are on stage, doubling on drums, trombone, saxophone and tenor banjo when they are recording. He and Alan are the keenest songwriters within the group, though they're often joined by Wayne.

Merrill told me that when the Osmonds are alone together, either travelling or at their homes in Utah and Los Angeles, they often discuss their future. "That comes up quite often," he said. "We are going to stay together as long as we can, and I know we're all hoping to branch out in different directions ... we have our own recording company now, and we'd also like to get into movie production.

"Alan and Wayne and I are already writing most of the songs the group records, and also Donny's B-sides

... and then I know Alan would also like to work as a producer, recording other acts, and so would Jay ... I'd like to become an actor, and also go to college in Utah ... that's why we have our main home now at Provo, right on the campus of the Brigham Young University. It means we could take up courses there if we wished.

"I expect we'll make a movie real soon, and that would be very exiting because none of us have done any acting before ... all sorts of ideas have been put forward, but the sort of thing we'd like to do would be a zany sort of espionage film, and then we would write the score if we could get round to doing it."

To Merrill, too, I also put questions about their religion, asking him whether he really thought it healthy to bring this so close to their music. "It's a way of life to us," he said. "We like it. We have loved it all our lives. Our families are all religious, and we were born and raised in Utah."

I also asked him whether he had any idea how much money the Osmonds were now grossing between them, with all those different sources of income. "That's something I don't really care to know, though I think we've done all right," said Merrill. "But we've paid a lot of tax ... our father takes care of all that ... we leave that to our mother and father, and then we give ten per cent of all we earn to the Church."

Like Alan, Merrill stressed the daily input of vitamins. "We're all very much into that," he said. "Wayne is very much that way – he's into all that organic stuff ... but I stick with the vitamins and cod liver oil, which our mother gives us every day because it's healthy."

When the Osmonds first came to Britain, Merrill quickly became one of the more popular members of the family – possibly because fans are quick to analyse a group's make-up and soon realise who is the most friendly, easy-going, responsive (and the reverse). So when he married last autumn, Fan Club Secretary Maureen Street had many letters asking her what his wife was like, how they met, about the marriage itself, and where they would make their home. She answered them in the next issue of the newsletter:

Question: When was Mary born?

Answer: July 19th, 1951.

Question: What colour hair and eyes does Mary have and how tall is she?

Answer: She has brown hair and brown eyes and she is 5ft 6in.

Question: When and where did they meet?

Answer: They met in late May on a blind date at the Sundance Restaurant in Utah. It was love at first sight.

Question: When did they get engaged?

Answer: A month before they were married.

Question: What subjects does Mary teach, and will she continue to work after becoming Mrs. M. Osmond?

Answer: Mary teaches all subjects, and will only tutor Jimmy, Donny and Marie privately now.

Question: How long did she train as a teacher?

Answer: She trained for four and a half years, and actually taught for four days – as it was at this time she and Merrill decided to marry.

Question: What time was the wedding, and was there a reception?

Answer: It was at 11 a.m. on September 17th at the Mormon Temple in Salt Lake City. There were so many people around "M & M" had to go through a tunnel under the church. The ceremony was only attended by close family and friends, and only Alan, Tommy and Virl actually attended the ceremony as they are the only members of the family (apart from Mr. and Mrs. Osmond of course) who have gone through the temple. They had a wedding breakfast afterwards at the Lyon House, which is a building belonging to the church, for 200 friends and relations. Another reception was held for them in Los Angeles, California, by their friend Mike Curb and manager Ed Leffler for all their Californian friends. This was Mary's first visit to California. When they get back to Utah another reception will be held in Mary's home town, Heber City, for their other Utah friends.

Question: What did Mary and Merrill wear at the wedding and who was the best man and bridesmaid?

Answer: Mary wore a plain white dress with a Spanish lace headdress. She looked incredibly lovely. For the ceremony Merrill wore a special white robe which is worn during a Mormon wedding ceremony and for the reception he wore a navy blue pin striped suit. There are no bridesmaids or best man at a Mormon wedding ceremony, and no flowers.

Question: Where will they live?

Answer: They have bought a three bedroomed house right next door to Virl. It's a Duplex style house.

Question: Do they want a family right away?

Answer: They do want a large family as they both have a love for children, but they are going to wait a while.

Question: What type of wedding rings do Mary and Merrill wear?

Answer: Mary has two bands of white gold connected by an arch on which sits a solitaire diamond. Merrill wears a white gold band.

Question: Does Mary like Merrill's fans?

Answer: Yes she does, and I know you all like her.

Question: What does Mary think of the Osmonds on stage?

Answer: Believe it or believe it not, Mary had never seen them on stage until they were married. She first saw them in cabaret in Las Vegas and of course enjoyed it. She said, "It felt strange to see my husband on stage and he was terrific."

As other members of the Osmonds marry and have children, probably settling in Utah where they clearly have the deepest roots, I would expect them to tour less and concentrate more on recording; in that new home in Provo they have their own studios in the basement, offices on the next floor, with a penthouse apartment above that.

This is an arrangement that makes them almost as self-sufficient in their work as they always used to be in childhood; soon, they will be able to produce their own masters at their studios in Provo (which is said to be even better equipped than most of the major companies' studios in Los Angeles), produce their own TV promotion films to accompany each record release, only having to leave Utah for major personal appearances.

"We are going to try to stay away from California," Merrill told me, just after the studios had been completed. "At the moment, that's where the business is and where our work is, but we'd like to get away from the whole racket ... and have a little more time for fishing and boating," he added in his easy-going way.

CHAPTER TWELVE

For hundreds of thousands of girl fans, Donny *is* the Osmonds. He is the one they scream for, standing in the street outside whichever hotel the family is staying in, standing there for hours on end even through pouring rain; he is their idol, their dreamboat.

Donny himself seems bemused by all this affection, almost embarrassed. "They're calling for you, Donny!" say his brothers, nudging his shoulder as he half-smiles, half-cringes. "Go on – go over to the window and wave," says Alan, and Donny seems to freeze.

One immediately forms the impression that all this adulation is overpowering. He stands there, just 5ft 7ins tall, a little over eight stone in weight, brown-haired and brown-eyed, hesitating. "He seems unbearably shy," says Maureen Street. "Donny was always a very serious little boy," says his father.

Donny was born the seventh son at 12.55 a.m. on Monday, December 9th, 1957, when the family were still living in their two-storeyed Ogden home behind the post office; a house which George Osmond – an expert carpenter – had expanded by boarding over the loft and turning it into a music and schoolroom for his children.

On the land attached to the house, with its large orchard, Mr. and Mrs. Osmond produced all their own fruit and vegetables; kept their own cow, Daisy, to provide the family with milk to make their butter and cheese – and their children were brought up to feel that they each had a job to do before going off to the Lincoln County school for the day. You will remember that in chapter two, I told you how Mrs. Osmond remembered, "We just had one cow, Daisy, who was the special responsibility of Virl and Tommy. She was very tame – and she was 'their' cow. They fed her, cleaned out her shed – and then every morning before going to school, they would milk her to provide milk for the family. One of the earliest memories I have of Donny is of him when he was still a toddler, sitting on the ground, cross-legged, playing while Virl and Tommy milked Daisy . . . it's just a little picture I have of him in my mind, sitting there."

When I asked them both how well they remembered him in childhood, Mr. and Mrs. Osmond paused and pondered. "It was a long time ago – and a lot has happened since then," said Mr. Osmond. "Remember, we've had nine children," he added, "so there was a lot happening around the house every day."

"Did we ever tell you about the peanut butter story?" asked Mrs. Osmond, and I said they hadn't. "Gosh, that was funny," said Mr. Osmond. "Donny was just a toddler then, three or four years old, and Marie was just a baby . . . one afternoon, Olive went out into the garden and left them sitting on the floor, playing . . . when she came back in, she had the shock of her life. They'd managed to get hold of a jar of peanut butter, and had started a 'fight'. It was all over their clothes, all over their faces, on the furniture and up the wall – you never saw such a mess. But there they were, sitting in the middle of it, happy as could be.

"Donny never really got into much mischief as a child. He was never that sort of boy. He was always very serious, and very determined . . . the first time he learned to walk, he really *worked* at it . . . and then when he started learning how to ride a bike and slide down on a toboggan, if he fell, he'd never cry. He'd just pick himself up, with his little jaw stuck out, and he'd start all over again . . . he always had this strong drive."

Later, after Alan, Wayne, Merrill and Jay had started appearing weekly on the Andy Williams TV series from 1962, the family moved out to California, making their first home in their Spanish-style hacienda, with its stone floors, swimming pool, and citrus fruit trees.

This is the period in his childhood of which Mr. and Mrs. Osmond seem to have the clearest recollection, possibly because they had given up their business interests in Ogden, and were now devoting all their energies to their children, helping Alan, Wayne, Merrill and Jay cope with their TV schedule; looking after their education; giving them as much normality as they could in their home life.

"Donny was a very curious little boy," Mrs. Osmond told me. "He used to follow his Dad around the house, watching everything he did . . . he and Alan were very much alike in that. He'd often just sit there, watching me working, whether I was ironing or cleaning the house . . . and I can remember once he plugged an extension cord from the iron into a socket in the wall, and then went and touched the iron with something, which gave him quite a 'bite' . . . it just shook him up a bit, and he didn't do that again.

"He always seemed to have this fascination for electricity, even when he was very young. For birthdays and at Christmas, we always used to buy him little battery-operated things because that would keep him happy for hours.

"He asked for my old razor box one day and turned

that into a telephone. And then he would make 'On' and 'Off' switches, and dimmers for lighting . . . he loved to just sit down in the middle of the floor taking clocks and engines and radios and things like that to pieces, and then putting them back together again.

"It's something that has stuck with him. In his bedroom, now he has his own workshop underneath his bed, and the bed itself is electrically operated so that he can press a switch, and it rises up on to a shelf leaving him free to work."

Donny told me himself that he had repaired radio and TV sets, had connected electric circuits to his stereo system so that different coloured lights would become projected as he played his albums, had built his own radio-controlled model plane, and had designed his own electric car (which he was planning to build).

At their apartment block in Los Angeles, he has built an internal telephone system linking every room – and he personally supervised the equipping of their two recording studios in Los Angeles and in the basement of their other home at Provo.

When the group are touring, Donny will check the wiring and earthing of their amplification system himself before they go out on stage – and when they are back in their hotel, you will find him tucked away in a corner, reading "Modern Electronics".

The hobby appears all-important, and he makes it a useful one – though a strange one for an international heart-throb. And it is not just a single-track enthusiasm – he is also a keen movie fan (especially of films starring Marlon Brando, Ryan O'Neal or Robert Redford), interested in most sports, and more accomplished in many of them than his brothers.

"He's always had this determination," says his father,

telling me at one point in our discussion that Donny was one of the best swimmers in the family, at another that he was good at skiing, and yet another that he was probably the finest horseman. And then academic subjects seem to interest him, too.

"I think we've probably worked harder than most kids do at school," Donny told me. "We have tutors and correspondence courses, and then our mother helps us ... I think education is very important to a person, and that's always been a feeling within our family. Our grandfather was a schoolteacher, and our grandmother on our mother's side was a teacher, too ... and then our uncle taught at college, and at one time our mother was going to be a teacher, so I guess we all have it in us."

This search for knowledge, which is an unexpected sidelight to the Osmond personna, continues no matter where they happen to be, no matter how wearing their schedule; during their British tours, Donny settled down every morning between 9 a.m. and noon for three hours of lessons with Marie and Jimmy before starting that day's round of interviews, photo sessions, TV taping and concert rehearsals.

This has now been his daily routine for most of the past four years; up to 1970, Donny just appeared occasionally on TV with his brothers – and it was only towards the end of that year that their recording career began. His own solo success only started in 1971 with the first million-seller "Sweet and Innocent", which was followed that year by "Hey Girl" and "Go Away Little Girl", and then in 1972 by "Puppy Love", "Too Young" and "Why", and then in 1973 by "Twelfth of Never", "Young Love" and "When I Fall in Love".

His first concerts with his brothers were not until May, 1971, and their first tour did not start until July of that year – so, in spite of those regular TV appearances with Andy Williams, their career in pop music has still been relatively short, and the pace at which they have worked has not been as punishing as the schedules undertaken by bands like Led Zeppelin, Grand Funk Railroad, Slade, the Sweet, Mott the Hoople, Black Sabbath, Yes, Ten Years After or any one of fifty other bands that often complete six or seven major tours a year. But it has still been tough for someone as young as Donny, who was only fourteen years old when he had his first hit record.

In that first year, 1971, he collapsed with acute appendicitis; in 1972, he fell ill in London with severe 'flu. And although his parents clearly take every precaution to minimise the strains, with the younger ones going to bed before 10 p.m. every night and eating to a sound diet, the schedule is still a hard one for a boy in his mid-teens – and in Jimmy's case, much younger.

"We literally live on the road," Donny told me when first we met in 1972. "So when we do have some free time, the last thing we want to do is go travelling . . . the tours are spaced out so that we can get back home to Utah for a month or so at a time, because that's our main home, and there's always so much to do there . . . at our ranch, we have our own lake up in the mountains where we keep a 20ft racing boat . . . we can go riding (we've got twenty-five horses), practise archery, go shooting . . . in the summer it's quite hot, but then in winter we have snow up there so we can go skiing . . . and we have so much more freedom there than we do anywhere else."

A sure sign that the pressure is not too hard is that Donny is always talking about the other things he would like to do in the future; ideas that he has obviously given some thought to. Already, he has learnt karate as a form of self-defence; he says he would like to learn shorthand and typing just for his own everyday convenience; that he would like to go on an electronics course, and that one day – perhaps if the Osmonds take a sabbatical year away from the music business – he says he would like to enrol as a student at the Brigham Young University to learn the theories of musical composition (his brother Alan has already taken a course in law, and Wayne a course in mathematics).

His father laughingly said to me during one of our discussions that he thought Donny would prove to be "another Edison", that he had this inventive interest in electronics, and that he and Wayne had both appeared "very clever" throughout childhood. One wonders how far this will go for he certainly seems to possess more undeveloped potential than his brothers, something those hundreds of thousands of girl fans have been quick to discern with their often remarkably shrewd intuitive sense.

CHAPTER THIRTEEN

Marie Osmond is one of the most envied girls in the world, yet not viciously so; the girl Osmond fans who meet her tend to regard Marie as more like an elder sister. "They're always very nice and friendly towards me, and write little notes for me to pass on to Donny," she says, and it is well known to them all that she and Donny are particularly close to each other.

Marie – her full name is Olive Marie Osmond – was born on October 13th, 1959, her father's brithday, when Donny was still less than two years old. With Alan, Wayne, Merrill and Jay away from home so often working on the Andy Williams TV series, she and Donny grew up particularly close to each other, and then when they were at home her older brothers tended to spoil her a little because she was the only girl in the family.

"My brothers have always been very protective towards me," she says, and when you meet them all together, this becomes very apparent; if she is in a corner of a room surrounded by journalists, they will quickly rescue her.

Marie is now 5ft 3in tall, and a little over eight stone in weight, with long brown hair and brown eyes, which she regrets ("I wish I'd been born with blue eyes," she says). For the past two years, she has occasionally joined her brothers on stage when they have been appearing in cabaret – and even appeared with them in concert at the Paris Olympia. In 1973, she had a No. 1 hit single in the States "Paper Roses", which was also a hit in Britain and Europe, and a successful country and western style album with the same title.

"But I'm still not sure whether I really want to pursue a solo career – or even a show business career," she says, mentioning that she would like to learn shorthand typing, that her main interests are jewellery and cooking, that she enjoys helping her mother with the family ironing and sewing, and that she would like to be able to design her own dresses. In the States, she has even given her name to a brand of organically produced "Marie Osmond Cosmetics", and there are plans to market these in this country. But still she says she is not sure whether show business is for her.

"It's a man's world," she says a little enigmatically, stressing that she believes her father is the patriach of the family, that everything in their lives is built around him, and that this is the correct basis for family life.

"The most important thing in your life is your family," she says, adding that she has never had a boyfriend since she accepts the parental dictum that no Osmond should start dating until the age of sixteen. "All my brothers accepted that, and I don't rebel against it ... we are a fantastic, crazy family ... my brothers are very protective towards me. Sure, I would like to have had another sister, though I reckon I've enjoyed being the only girl in the family ... now, I've got a 'sister' since Merrill married, because Mary travels with us everywhere, and we go shopping together ... I enjoy being with Mary because most of my other friends are back home in Utah and I only see them when I'm there ... I'd never thought of being a singer until a year ago, and now I've found I like it, and I really love singing; getting up on stage and joining in is fun, but I don't know whether I want to make a career of it ...

if I do, then my mother will travel with me everywhere. She came down to Nashville with me when we recorded the album there, and I'd like her to travel with me if ever I toured on my own.

"The No. 1 priority for a song for me is that it should be easy to listen to," says Marie, emphasising that she is primarily a country and western style singer, and that therefore her songs appeal to a slightly older audience, to boys and girls between the ages of eighteen and twenty-five. "It is definitely an older audience," she says, adding that she likes the Carpenters herself, and that David Cassidy is "O.K."

She says she has never taken voice lessons, has written one song with Donny, learned karate with her brothers ("just so that I would be able to defend myself"), and returns again to the subject of the Osmonds' life together as a family. "We may pursue our careers in different ways, but we will never break up as a family," she says, sounding quaintly old fashioned, but a very good Mormon as she continues:

"I believe a woman's place is in the home. As for Women's Lib – well, I am sure a lot of people like it, but personally I do not feel that it is for me. Every girls' ultimate ambition is to get married and raise a family, and that's mine . . . the time will come when someone feels that they are right for me, and I feel the same about them.

"My brothers are very good to me. Alan is the big brother sort of brother, who helps with all my problems. He is the one who will be first to notice if I am wearing a new dress, and will say something nice about it . . . Wayne helps me with my scriptures. Every day I read a passage from the Book of Mormon, and he gives me a question and answer session to make sure that I have remembered it right. He is very serious and thoughtful... Merrill is crazy, really neat – and marriage has not changed him at all ... Jay is the same, quite crazy, the joker of the family – and some of them are pretty bad!... Donny is the one that I am closest to, probably because we are closest in age, and used to play together in the back yard ... Jimmy is really cool.

"We're a very close family. I help my mother with a lot of the work at home, and now we want to design all my clothes together ... sewing is one of my hobbies, but I just don't get enough time ... I do all my own packing, and have developed a system so that clothes don't get too creased when we are travelling, tucking things away in the corners ... when we were in London, Mary and I went to Biba's and that was fantastic – and we loved Way In at Harrods.

"We went there on our own during the day, and a few girls recognised us – but they were all very nice. They don't chase us and scream like they would if they saw Donny. They asked me about him, and gave me little messages for him, when I got back to the hotel, which I gave him, of course.

"My brothers all treat me. I'm very indulged. If I see something I like, they will probably buy it for me ... I don't think of them as stars. They are just my brothers, and we have a lot of fun together ... the only time we ever get worried is when the fans start climbing over the roof of our car, or something like that. That's why we have so much security around us – so that we don't get hurt, and neither do they ... but that's the only real worry we have ... the rest of the time it's fun, great fun, because we all love being together."

CHAPTER FOURTEEN

A large question mark now hangs over the Osmonds. At the beginning of 1974, after Mike Curb had left MGM Records, the Osmonds started legal proceedings against the record company, as a result of which the supply of tapes to Polydor in London ceased. "We don't know what it's all about since we haven't been told," a Polydor spokesman told "Record Mirror" on February 22nd. "The Osmonds records we release have to go through MGM and at the moment we're not getting any tapes."

This meant that the album the Osmonds were plannine to record in the first two months of 1974 had to be shelved, though this is a problem that many groups have had to overcome in the past – but temporarily it meant that no release dates could be given for the next singles from Donny and Marie, and for the group's own singles, though in mid-March Jimmy Osmond's single "I'm Going To Knock On Your Door" was issued in Britain. The news was not greeted with dismay in the British music papers: the "New Musical Express" even thought its readers would be grateful that for the moment the sound of the Osmonds had been stilled!

For lesser groups, a dispute with a record company can be fatal, because they so often depend on the company for their finance – with advances on royalties paying for their equipment, for a weekly wage for each member of the group, and for their recording costs. No such problem confronts the Osmonds. They have their own recording studio in Los Angeles, which has already been used by Bread and the British group Springfield Revival, as well as their own studio in Provo, Utah, where they also have their own business headquarters in that three-story building remodelled by brother Virl.

And their financial independence is not in doubt; quite apart from their recording income over the past three years, The Osmonds signed a four-year contract in February, 1974, guaranteeing them one million dollars a year to appear for a maximum of eight weeks a year at the Tropicana Hotel in Las Vegas (Tom Jones and Engelbert Humperdinck have signed similar long term Las Vegas cabaret contracts in the past).

Much more worrying for the Osmonds must have been their reception in Britain on their autumn tour in 1973; superficially, it was a success – but the accident at the airport cast a shadow over the tour, and made several papers question the way their arrival at Heathrow was advertised in advance. Both on television and at their press conferences, Alan found himself on the defensive; when the question came up at the conference I attended (see chapter nine) the tension was apparent, as the others listened with solemn faces while Alan criticised the press photographers for their coverage of the scenes at the airport.

But even more questionable than this (and this, too, was an undercurrent at the press conferences) is the relationship between the Osmonds and the Mormon Church, for this is the first time that a major group has so openly drawn attention to its religion in an almost ambassadorial way.

There have been other pop stars who have been influenced by different religions, notably Elvis Presley, Little Richard, Gilbert O'Sullivan, David Bowie,

Peter Hope-Evans of Medicine Head, George Harrison and Pete Townshend since the days when Terry Dene gave up pop music to become a kerbside evangelist, and one of the Shadows became a Jehovah's Witness. And then there has been Cliff Richard who, after quietly helping to run a youth club in Finchley for some years, publicly turned to religion, and has since taken part in international crusades, appeared with Billy Graham, made an evangelical film, toured church youth clubs and spoken and played at school prize days, even associating himself with Lord Longford.

What has been so different about the Osmonds is that firstly they have been so successful in so many areas of pop music, and secondly they have consistently stressed the importance of their religion both in their work, in their home and in their everyday lives; it's a theme that permeates the conversations of their father George Osmond, who was a Bishop in the Church back home in Utah – and they remind you that Virl and Tommy have both been missionaries, that Alan and Merrill are both elders of the Church, and that the younger members of the family daily read their scriptures.

That is not to say that there is anything wrong in this, but it does seem strange to read in a fan club newsletter paragraphs like this:

> "You have asked me many questions about the Mormon religion. Please can you write direct to the branch of the Church here, where the Elders will be glad to help. The address is: The Church of Jesus Christ of Latter Day Saints, 64/68 Princes Gate, Exhibition Road, London, SW7, 2PA."

or this:

> "The address of the Mormon Church in Britain, if you are interested in the serious side of our boys,

is The Church of Jesus Christ of Latter Day Saints, 64/68 Exhibition Road, London, SW7 2PA (sic). (Make sure you send an SAE if you want details) . . ."

or this:

"THE SERIOUS SIDE OF OUR FAMILY

I have received thousands upon thousands of letters asking me about the Mormon Church, as you know I have told you where to write but for the benefit of new members who are truly interested in obtaining details, the Book of Mormon or "The Pearl of Great Price" (this book is part of the scriptures) can write to President Milan D. Smith, The Church of Jesus Christ of Latter Day Saints, 64/68 Exhibition Road, South Kensington, SW7. He will be glad to help, but you must send a SAE . . ."

And then there were the religious overtones to Merrill's wedding (see chapter eleven), and the overt message-bringing of the Osmond's album, "The Plan".

This is not to suggest that there is anything sinister in all this. Indeed, the Osmonds are quite open about their religion; they say they have been given time off from what would have been missionary work to concentrate on their music, and they are undoubtedly exemplary in every aspect of their lives; loving their parents, advocating the virtues of family life; spurning immorality and alcohol, drugs and coffee, and even Coca Cola, and placing such stress upon education and self-improvement.

But should there be this sort of influence in pop music. Does the very fact that pop music is the medium of the young make it a little vulnerable?

I leave the reader to form his or her own opinion.

Certainly, for my part I have found all those members of the Osmond family that I have met to be exceptionally friendly, better educated than many people in pop music, both academically and as musicians, and their success is little short of phenomenal; no other family has produced four separate acts, each appealing to a different age group.

In a material sense, the Osmonds must have become one of the wealthiest families in the history of entertainment; remember – they acquired that 2,300-acre ranch and that herd of Simenthal cattle *before* they started making hit singles and albums, *before* their success in Japan, Europe, Australasia, Britain and the United States.

Now, they have their own recording studios in Los Angeles and Provo, their production company, their marketing operation, the Marie Osmond range of cosmetics, the Mrs. Osmond cookery book, their stage tours, their stake in the British magazine "Osmonds World", their fan club, their record sales, their Performing Rights income every time one of those records is played on radio or TV, their songwriting income, their fees from concerts and personal appearances.

They have their investments in real estate, that apartment building in Los Angeles where they live when working on the West Coast, that three-storey office-cum-home in Provo, and their original home in Ogden, Utah.

And it can hardly be said that the Osmonds have been selfish, though they are undoubtedly good businessmen; ten per cent of all they earn has gone to their Church, and other money has been channelled into The Osmond Foundation, which is a non profit-making trust to provide funds for the education of deaf and blind children.

And they have done all this as a family, a remarkably ordinary family at heart employing just a small road crew when they are touring – but no maids, no cooks, no house-keepers, no personal staff. All the minutiae of everyday life are looked after by Mrs. Osmond and Marie – plus their modern armoury of micro wave ovens, sewing machines, electric grills, meat grinders, wheat grinders, fruit juicers and vegetable presses.

"Natural foods every day," decrees Mrs. Osmond. "Plenty of meat, vegetables and natural juices – with no artificial additives, no colouring, and no chemicals."

She once told me that their whole life as a family had been based on a dictum by the world famous American architect Frank Lloyd Wright – "Clean living, high thinking, plain cooking."

This may not suit everyone. But it has worked for the Osmonds.

CHRONOLOGY

1917	
October 13	George Osmond born at Etna, Wyoming.
1925	
May 4	Olive Davis born at Samaria, Idaho.
1944	
December 1	George Osmond marries Olive Davis at the Mormon Temple, Salt Lake City.
1945	
October 26	Tommy Osmond born.
1947	
October 19	Virl Osmond born.
1949	
June 22	Alan Ralph Osmond born.
1951	
July 19	Mary Osmond (Merrill's wife) born.
August 28	Wayne Osmond born.
1953	
April 30	Merrill Davis Osmond born.
1955	
March 2	Jay Wesley Osmond born.
1957	
December 9	Donald Clark Osmond – Donny – born.
1959	
October 13	Olive Marie Osmond born.
1960	
	Osmond brothers try for audition with Lawrence Welk. Family buys holiday home in Northern Utah.
1962	
	Osmond Brothers begin weekly TV series with Andy Williams which runs for four years. The family buy a home near Los Angeles.

1963	
April 16	James Arthur Osmond (Little Jimmy) born.
	Osmond Brothers appear in TV special "The Seven Little Foys", and make TV series "The Travels of Jamie McPheeters" with actor Kurt Russell.
1966	
	Osmond Brothers appear regularly on TV series "The Jerry Lewis Show".
1968	
	Jimmy becomes first Osmond to have a hit record – at the age of five, and in Japan. The record is "My Little Darling".
December 21	Virl Osmond marries wife Chris.
1969	
	Osmond Brothers rejoin Andy Williams to make another year-long TV series.
October 31	Aaron Osmond born, son of Virl.
1970	
March	The Osmond Brothers tour Japan and on their return to the U.S. they sign a recording Contract with MGM.
November 1	Jared Osmond born, son of Virl.
December	Osmond Brothers have their first hit, "One Bad Apple", which goes to No. 1 in U.S. Charts. Film TV special "The Osmond Brothers" and record first LP, from which Donny's track "Sweet and Innocent" is later released as a single. Spend Christmas in Japan.
1971	
March	Osmonds again tour Japan, where they meet Masanobu Ono, who has been their road manager ever since.

May 28	Osmonds make first headlining concert appearance at Cleveland, Ohio.
29	Second concert appearance at Columbus, Ohio.
30	Third concert appearance at Houston, Texas.
June–Sept	Osmonds spend June at their ranch at Wartske, Utah, and then begin first nation-wide U.S. tour, playing concerts in 48 cities.
September 24	Donny nearly dies of acute appendicitis.
1972	
January 13	Tommy Osmond marries wife Lyn.
January	Osmonds' first trip to Britain has to be postponed when Wayne enters hospital for hernia operation.
April 15	Virginia Osmond born, daughter of Virl.
May 19	Osmonds fly to London for first British appearance.
22	Osmonds tape ATV Royal Gala at the London Palladium in aid of the British Olympic Team Appeal Fund. Afterwards, they meet the Queen and Duke of Edinburgh.
28	ATV Royal Gala Show televised.
May–June	Osmonds have their first hit single in Britain "Down By The Lazy River", and then Donny has No. 1 hit with "Puppy Love".
August–September	Donny has second hit "Too Young".
September	Osmonds appear in cabaret at Caesar's Palace, Las Vegas.
October 29	Osmonds fly to London. Huge crowds at airport. Go direct to Churchill Hotel for press conference.

30	Osmonds appear on BBC-1 programme "Nationwide". Donny guests on Jimmy Young's Radio One show.
November 1	Osmonds film "Crazy Horses" for "Top Of The Pops". Donny films "Why".
2	Osmonds film four songs for London Weekend TV show.
3	MGM release "Long Haired Lover From Liverpool" (Jimmy Osmond), "Why" (Donny Osmond) and "Crazy Horses" (Osmonds).
4	Donny guests on Ed Stewart's Radio One programme "Junior Choice". Osmonds make first British concert appearance at Rainbow Theatre, London.
6	Osmonds in concert at the Free Trade Hall, Manchester.
7	Osmonds in concert at Town Hall, Birmingham.
9	Osmonds' second concert at the Rainbow.
13	Osmonds fly from Heathrow to Bremen.
14	Osmonds film German TV special.
15	Osmonds fly from Bremen to Amsterdam.
16	Dutch TV show.
17–21	Fly from Amsterdam to Paris for concert at Paris Olympia and two French TV shows.
December	Osmonds' album "Crazy Horses" released here by MGM.
8	"Osmonds Live At The Rainbow" screened on BBC-1.
16	Benjamin Thomas Osmond born, son of Tommy.

1973

January 1	European Fan Club formed with Maureen Street as its secretary.
	Jimmy Osmond's album "Killer Joe" released.
February 28–March 5	Alan and Donny fly to London with their father, also visiting Germany and Holland. Receive special trophy from Polydor for selling over £1,000,000-worth of records in 1972.
March 5	Donny's single "Twelfth of Never"/"Life Is Just What You Make It" (MGM).
	Album "The Plan" recorded by the Osmonds in Los Angeles.
21	Osmonds present their stage show to a convention of Congressmen and record industry executives in Washington.
23	Jimmy's single "Tweedlee Dee"/"Mama'd Know What To Do" (MGM).
March 23–April 4	Osmonds appear at Caesar's Palace, Las Vegas, supported by Rich Little and the Ding A Lings.
April	Appear in cabaret at Lake Tahoe, Nevada.
April 30	Osmonds record Japanese TV soft drinks commercial, "Calpis".
May	Donny's album "Alone Together" released (MGM).
June 6	Osmonds single "Goin' Home"/"Are You Up There?" (MGM)
August 3	Begin major U.S. concert tour with Springfield Revival at Allentown Fair, Pennsylvania.
4	Second day at Allentown Fair.
7	Civic Arena, Pittsburgh.
8	Convention Centre, Cleveland, Ohio.

9	Memorial Auditorium, Buffalo, New York.
10	Donny's single "Young Love"/"A Million To One" released (MGM). Osmonds at Cobo Hall, Detroit, Michigan.
11	Cincinatti Gardens, Ohio.
13	The Comni, Atlanta, Georgia.
14	Garrett Coliseum, Montgomery, Alabama.
15	Legion Field, Birmingham, Alabama.
16	Mid South Coliseum, Memphis, Tennessee.
17	Municipal Auditorium, Nashville, Tennessee.
18	State Fair, Indianapolis, Indiana – Alan breaks Jay's nose during stage karate routine.
20	State Fair, Des Moines, Iowa.
21	ditto.
22	Municipal Auditorium, Kansas City, Missouri.
24	Arlington Park, Chicago.
25	Fair du Quinon, Illinois.
27	Ohio State Fair.
28	ditto.
September 17	Merrill marries Mary Carlson at the Mormon Temple, Salt Lake City.
September 20 (to October 10)	Osmonds in cabaret at Caesar's Palace, Las Vegas.
22	Riots at Rainbow Theatre, London, when tickets go on sale for Osmonds concert.
October 19	Osmonds' single "Let Me In"/"One Way Ticket to Anywhere" (MGM). Osmonds fly to Gothenburg, Sweden, at start of European tour.
20	Concert at KB Hall, Copenhagen.
21	Osmonds arrive in London.

23	Concert at Belle Vue, Manchester.
25	Concert at Apollo, Glasgow.
27	Concert at Rainbow Theatre, London. Osmonds on Ed Stewart's programme "Junior Choice" (Radio One).
30	Concert for fan club members only at Rainbow Theatre, London.
31	Osmonds fly to Paris.
November 2	Concert at Arens, Antwerp. Donny's single "Are You Lonesome Tonight"/ "When I Fall in Love" released in Britain (MGM).
3	Concert at Groenoordhal, Rotterdam.
5	Concert at Jahrhunderthalle, Frankfurt.
6	Concert at Deutschlandhalle, Berlin.
7	Concert at Congress Centrum, Hamburg.
9	Marie Osmond's single "Paper Roses"/ "Least Of All You" and her album released in Britain (MGM).
December	Donny's album "A Time For Us" released in Britain.
1974	
January 16	TV documentary "On Tour With the Osmonds" shown on BBC-1.
25	Announced that the Osmonds have been contracted to appear eight weeks a year at the Tropicana Hotel, Las Vegas, for the next four years for 1,000,000 U.S. dollars a year.
February 8	Jimmy Osmond single "I'm Gonna Knock On Your Door" (MGM).
July 12–August 1	Osmonds make first appearance at Tropicana Hotel, Las Vegas, under their four-year contract.

Enterprise Stardust

PERILOUS DAWN . . .

Major Perry Rhodan, commander of the spaceship STARDUST, found more than anyone had expected might exist on the moon — for he became the first man to make contact with another sentient race!

The Arkonides had come from a distant star, and they possessed a knowledge of science and philosophy that dwarfed mankind's knowledge.

But these enormously powerful alien beings refused to cooperate with the people of Earth . . . unless Perry Rhodan could pass the most difficult test any human being had ever faced . . .

ENTERPRISE STARDUST is the first novel in the Perry Rhodan series which sold more than 70 million copies in Europe and America.

The Radiant Dome

CHALLENGE FROM THE STARS . . .

Perry Rhodan had returned from the moon in Spaceship Stardust accompanied by two of the Arkonides. But the earth was on the verge of an atomic conflict. So Perry Rhodan, Peacelord of the Universe, threw an impregnable forcefield around the Stardust and declared his ship independent of the warring nations.

As he had hoped, the holocaust was temporarily averted by the more deadly threat of his allies from the stars; but could Perry Rhodan keep the peace long enough to persuade the Arkonides that mankind was fit to enter their galactic community?

THE RADIANT DOME is the second novel in the world's bestselling S.F. series. Don't miss Perry Rhodan's first cosmic adventure, ENTERPRISE STARDUST.

The Face in the Abyss

A remote valley hidden amid the towering peaks of the Andes and never before visited by civilised man is the scene of A. A. Merritt's classic novel of supernatural fantasy. The valley is inhabited by creatures long forgotten and races pledged to the resurrection of the glorious past.

Into this valley stumbles a young mining engineer, Nicholas Graydon. He defies the commands of the Snake-Mother's invisible but deadly servants and returns to the forbidden valley for the sake of Suarra, whom he loves. But Suarra can not be his until Graydon has persuaded the Snake-Mother to free the land of Yu-Atlanchi from Nimir, the Shadow of Evil. And the way to the Snake-Mother is beset with perils. Such as Lantlu, rider of dinosoaurs; the Lizard men. And, of course, the Dark Lord himself.

The Face in the Abyss

A remote valley hidden amid the towering peaks of the Andes and never before visited by civilised man is the scene of A. A. Merritt's classic novel of supernatural fantasy. The valley is inhabited by creatures long forgotten and races pledged to the resurrection of the glorious past.

Into this valley stumbles a young mining engineer, Nicholas Graydon. He defies the commands of the Snake-Mother's invisible but deadly servants and returns to the forbidden valley for the sake of Suarra, whom he loves. But Suarra can not be his until Graydon has persuaded the Snake-Mother to free the land of Yu-Atlanchi from Nimir, the Shadow of Evil. And the way to the Snake-Mother is beset with perils. Such as Lantlu, rider of dinosoaurs; the Lizard men. And, of course, the Dark Lord himself.

Dwellers in the Mirage

Beneath the shimmering surface of a lake cradled in the desolate Alaskan mountains, the people of the Shadowed-Land waited for Dwayanu, the warrior hero who will bring back to the world the worship of Khalk'ru, the cruel, destructive octopus god whose appetites must be appeased by human sacrifice.

When Lief Langdon accidentally discovers the people beneath the valley floor, they welcome him as the reincarnation of Dwayanu. Slowly Langdon's personality is possessed by the pride and blood-lust of his warrior ancestor until he is driven by forces beyond his understanding or control to serve the evil power of Khalk'ru.

A classic of science fiction, DWELLERS IN THE MIRAGE weaves a powerful web of fantasy against a background of lost civilisations.

NOW A STUNNING WARNER BROS FILM STARRING LUCILLE BALL

MAME Patrick Dennis

"Few books so fully justify the cliche, 'a laugh in every line'. " *BIRMINGHAM MAIL*

"A regular Japanese doll of a woman had strolled into the foyer. Her hair was very short with straight bangs above her slanting brows . . . she had the longest fingernails I had ever seen, each lacquered a delicate green. An almost endless bamboo cigarette holder hung languidly from her bright red mouth. Somehow she looked vaguely familiar . . . There was a moment's silence. 'But darling,' she said dramatically, '*I'm* your Auntie Mame!'."

And the Japanese look was only one of Auntie Mame's innumerable poses, as Patrick Dennis soon discovered when she adopted him at the age of ten. Because whenever Auntie Mame went bankrupt or felt at all depressed, she simply dyed her hair a different colour and changed her image. Which made life exhilarating, but extremely exhausting.

"As finely feathered an heiress as ever believed in progressive education and gin." – *SUNDAY TIMES*